NORTHER

presei

C000090790

BREAK AWAY

by Dameon Garnett

First performed at the Finborough Theatre
on Tuesday 1 March 2005

Break Away

by Dameon Garnett

Cast in order of appearance

Barbie-Jean	**Claire Sundin**
Jake	**Gareth Llewelyn**
Kevin	**Colin R Campbell**
Stella	**Emily Norman**
Pauline	**Tina Malone**

Directed by	**Claire Lovett**
Designed by	**Paul Wills**
Lighting by	**Gavin Owen**
Sound Design by	**Emma Laxton**
Costumes by	**Jackie Orton**
Stage Managed by	**Daniel Staniforth**

The action takes place in Speke, Liverpool, and Torquay, Devon, in 2002

There will be one interval of fifteen minutes.

The performance lasts approximately two hours.

Our patrons are respectfully reminded that, in this intimate theatre, any noise such as rustling programmes, talking or the ringing of mobile phones may distract the actors and your fellow audience-members.

A unisex toilet – including a disabled toilet – is located on the ground floor. Separate toilet facilities for Ladies and Gentlemen are located on the basement level.

Interval drinks may be ordered in advance from the bar.

First performance at the Finborough Theatre
Tuesday 1 March 2005

Cast

Colin R Campbell Kevin

Colin R Campbell's many credits include *Having A Ball* (Birmingham Rep/ National Tour), *Othello* (York Theatre Royal), *A View From The Bridge* (Crucible, Sheffield), *Richard III* (German Tour), *Anna Karenina* (Theatre Royal Plymouth), *'Tis Pity She's A Whore* (Derby Playhouse), *When We Are Married* (Savoy Theatre), *Three Cheers For Mrs Butler* (Polka Theatre), *The Jaws of Darkness*, *Temple* and *Home Free!* (Orange Tree), *Macbeth* (English Touring Theatre), *Omma* (Young Vic), *Adam And Eve* (The Gate), *Bremmen Coffee* (Grove Theatre), *Pawnbroker Hocks The Moon, The Ragged Trousered Philanthropists* and *Dancing In The Dark* (all for the Metro Theatre Company), *Keeper's Bitter* and *Don't Let Your Babies Grow Up To Be Cowboys*. (both Pentabus Theatre Company) and many shows for Barrie Rutter's Northern Broadsides: *Richard III, The Merry Wives of Windsor, Antony and Cleopatra, Romeo and Juliet* and *The Passion*. TV includes *Casualty, Single, Heartbeat, Out Of Sight, Touch And Go, The Darling Buds of May, Love Hurts* and *The Bill*.

Gareth Llewelyn Jake

Recently graduated from the Central School of Speech and Drama and made his professional debut in the role of Little Monk in *Becket* (Theatre Royal, Haymarket). Roles in training included Flute in *A Midsummer Night's Dream*, Cyril in *Absolute Hell*, Mangolis in *The Kitchen*, Shapkin in *The Storm*, Aeneas in *Troilus and Cressida*, Witwoud in *The Way of the World*, Jake in *A Lie of the Mind* and Arragon/Old Gobbo in *The Merchant of Venice*.

Tina Malone Pauline

Trained with the Rathbone Theatre Company and went on to form Wisecrack, an all-female theatre company in Liverpool where she wrote, directed and produced. Her many credits include *The Word* (National Tour) for which she was nominated for the Best Actress Award in the *Manchester Evening News* Awards 2002, *Guiding Star* (Royal National Theatre), *Waiting For H* (Liverpool Everyman), *Running For Cover* (Liverpool Playhouse) and *Masquerade, Sentimental Journey, Cartoon Capers, Lux 2, A Spoonful Of Sugar* and *Maralade's Magic* (all for the Rathbone Theatre Company). TV includes *Shameless, Henry VIII, Nice Guy Eddie, Starhunter, Tough Love, Dinnerladies, Nature Boy, Something for the Weekend, The Harry Enfield Show, Common as Muck, Sin Bin* and Mo McGee in *Brookside*. Films include *Comfort Zone, Married To Malcolm, Livertonian, Long Day Closes, Blonde First* and Willy Russell's *Terraces*.

Emily Norman Stella

Emily Norman's most recent credits include Anne Garland in *The Trumpet Major* (The Bridewell), Elaine Robinson in *The Graduate* (Gielgud Theatre), Steph in *Never Saw The Day* (Irish Tour), *Emma* (Norwich Playhouse),

Tess of the D'Urbervilles (National Tour) and *Ladies In Retirement* (Chelsea Theatre). TV includes Laura in *Urban Species* (Channel 5) and Amelia in *A Ghost Of Christmas Past*.

Claire Sundin Barbie-Jean

Claire Sundin recently graduated from The Liverpool Institute for Performing Arts where she performed as Helen Hobart in *Once in A Lifetime,* Sarah in *Company,* Hester in *Equus* and in Jason Robert Brown's *Songs for a New World*. Other Theatre includes *Starting Now* (NSTC at the Edinburgh Festival), *Godspell* (National Tour) and with Theatre of the Wheel (Devon and Cornwall Tour). She has been involved in workshopping new writing at the Live Theatre, The Venue and the Soho Theatre.

Production

Dameon Garnett Playwright

Dameon Garnett was born in Liverpool. *Break Away* is his first produced play. His play, *New Year's Day*, was given a staged reading at the Royal Court Young Writers' Festival, starring Michael Angelis. He was an Associate Writer at the Liverpool Everyman, and has also received a bursary from the Soho Theatre. He has had staged readings of his plays performed at the New Ambassador's, the ICA and the Pleasance, all directed by Rufus Norris. One of his plays was workshopped at The Bush and he was invited by the Chelsea Theatre to develop a new play, *Living*, subsequently performed there as a staged reading.

Claire Lovett Director

Claire Lovett was Assistant Director to Terry Johnson on *The Dumb Show* (Royal Court), to Lindsay Posner on *Oleanna* (Garrick Theatre), to Thea Sharrock on *A Doll's House* (Southwark Playhouse) and to Rufus Norris on *Dirty Butterfly* (Soho Theatre). Claire has also worked extensively as a stage manager at the Royal Court Theatre, Soho Theatre, The Bush, Theatre Clwyd Cymru and Lincoln Center, New York.

Paul Wills Designer

Design credits include *Breathing Corpses* (Royal Court – written by Laura Wade, Pearson Writer-in-Residence at the Finborough Theatre) *Gompers* and *References to Salvador Dali Make Me Hot* (Arcola Theatre), *Car Thieves* (Birmingham Rep), *Battina and the Moon* (Crucible Studio), *The School of Night* (RSC at The Other Place), *Lord of the Flies* (St Paul's, Hammersmith) and *Young Voices* (Sheffield Theatres Education tour).

Gavin Owen Lighting

Gavin Owen is currently part of the lighting team at the Royal Court. Designs at the Royal Court include *The Weather, Bear Hug, The One with the Oven, Just a Bloke, Night Owls, Kingswood Kids, Porcelain, The Canvas* and *Sugar*. He was Associate Designer on *Hitchcock Blonde* (Lyric Theatre) and *Lucky Dog* (Royal Court). His other credits include *Cross Purposes* (Union Theatre), *The Matchgirls* and *Mack and Mabel* (Palace Theatre, Watford), *Splinters* and *My Passionate Madness* (Massa Dance Company), *Blue Murder* and *Jacknife* (Telltale Theatre Company).

Emma Laxton Sound Designer

Emma Laxton is Sound Deputy at the Royal Court where she has worked as a sound designer on *Bone, The Weather, Bear Hug Terrorism* and *Food Chain*. Other Theatre includes *The Unthinkable* (Crucible Studio, Sheffield), *My Dad is a Birdman* (Young Vic), *Party Time* and *One for the Road* (BAC), *As You Like It* and *Romeo and Juliet* (Open Air Theatre, Regent's Park).

finboroughtheatre

Founded in 1980 – and celebrating its 25th anniversary in 2005 – the Finborough Theatre presents new writing from the UK and overseas (particularly from the USA, Canada and Ireland), music theatre and rediscoveries from 1850 onwards, many produced by our resident company, Concordance.

In its first decade, names connected with the theatre included Clive Barker, Kathy Burke, Ken Campbell, Mark Rylance and Clare Dowie (the world premiere of *Adult Child/Dead Child*). From 1991–94, new plays included Naomi Wallace's first play *The War Boys;* Rachel Weisz in David Farr's *Neville Southall's Washbag* which later became the West End play, *Elton John's Glasses*; and three plays by Anthony Neilson – *The Year of the Family; Normal: the Dusseldorf Ripper;* and *Penetrator* which transferred from the Traverse and went on to play at the Royal Court Upstairs.

From 1994, the theatre was run by The Steam Industry, winners of the Guinness Award in 1996 and 1997. Highlights included Tony Marchant's *The Fundraisers*; David Eldridge's *A Week with Tony*; Howard Goodall's musical *The Hired Man*; *Crime and Punishment*, shortlisted for the Empty Space Peter Brook Award; and new writing development which included Mark Ravenhill's *Shopping and F***king* (Royal Court, West End and New York), Naomi Wallace's *Slaughter City* (RSC) and David Eldridge's *Serving It Up* (The Bush). Other productions included the British premiere of David Mamet's *The Woods*, and Anthony Neilson's *The Censor*, which transferred to the Royal Court.

Neil McPherson became Artistic Director in 1999. Productions included Brad Fraser's *Wolfboy* (*Time Out* Critics Choice); Chris Pickles' *The Silent Treatment* (one of *Theatre Record*'s Top 10 Plays of 2001); Liz Phelps' *Modern Dance for Beginners,* subsequently produced at the Soho Theatre; the UK premiere of Lanford Wilson's *Sympathetic Magic* (*Time Out* Critics' Choice); Paulo Coelho's *The Alchemist*; Carolyn Scott-Jeffs' sell-out comedy *Out in the Garden* (which transferred to the Assembly Rooms, Edinburgh) and *Tarnished Angel* (subsequently broadcast on BBC Radio); Chris Dunkley's *Mirita* (*Time Out* Critics' Choice); the musical *Schwartz It All About*; the London premiere of Larry Kramer's *The Destiny of Me*

(Nicholas de Jongh's No 1 Critics Choice in *The Evening Standard*); and Louise Page's *Falkland Sound*.

The theatre reopened after a six month refurbishment in 2003. Since then, productions included Time Out Critics' Choices for the UK premiere of Tennessee Williams' *Something Cloudy, Something Clear,* Sonja Linden's *I Have Before Me a Remarkable Document Given to Me by a Young Lady from Rwanda*, the specially commissioned adaptation of W H Davies' *Young Emma* by Laura Wade (winner of the Pearson Award as our writer-in-residence) and directed by Tamara Harvey, Jason Hall's *Eyes Catch Fire*, Lynn Siefert's *Coyote Ugly*, the first London revival for more than 40 years of Rolf Hochhuth's *Soldiers*, and William Gaunt and John Bennett in the UK Premiere of Frank McGuinness' *Gates of Gold*. Other productions have included *The Women's War* – a centenary celebration of the suffragette movement; Steve Hennessy's *Lullabies of Broadmoor* on the Finborough Road murder of 1922; the Victorian comedy *Masks and Faces*; Amy Evans' *Achidi J's Final Hours*; and the fourth professional production in the UK of Giles Cooper's *Happy Family*. In 2004, the theatre was named as one of *Variety's* top five London fringe venues, and won the Empty Space Peter Brook Award Mark Marvin Award.

Our website includes more theatre history, reviews of previous productions, a history of the local area and details of our Friends Scheme at www.finboroughtheatre.co.uk

For Northern Edge

Northern Edge would like to thank Portsmouth Grammar School, Dr Tim Hands, Sandy Sullivan, James Priory, Jan Webber, Christine Rogers, Christine Giles, Alistair Norgate and David Hampshire, Jonathan Lloyd, Janette Smith, Marie and Jo at Clapham Community Project, Tansy Blaike, Lisa Makin, Sue Bird, Nicki Brown and Kelli Marsden, Stick, Dan Lockett, Jenny Livsey and Nicki Welburn, Amanda Radfern, Richard Ward, Paul and Marco at ALLSET, Louise Lovett and Hannah Dickinson.

In loving memory of Sheila Garnett, 1933–1984

BREAK AWAY

First published in 2005 by Oberon Books Ltd
521 Caledonian Road, London N7 9RH
Tel: 020 7607 3637 / Fax: 020 7607 3629
e-mail: oberon.books@btconnect.com
www.oberonbooks.com

A catalogue record for this book is available from the British
Library.

ISBN: 1 84002 549 2

Printed in Great Britain by Antony Rowe Ltd, Chippenham

CHARACTERS

BARBIE-JEAN

JAKE

KEVIN

STELLA

PAULINE

Act 1

Speke, Liverpool. Friday evening, 5pm. School has just broken up for the summer holiday. A bedroom. BARBIE-JEAN, aged 17, is attending to her hair in the mirror, meticulously spraying it: it is a mass of tight black ringlets, lobbed over to one side. She is wearing a white shell-suit, too small for her chubby physique. Her skin is over-tanned. The room is very 'girly' but also very ordered and tidy, with a dresser, bed, cuddly-toy, telephone, basket and desk. On the wall is an enormous poster of a young Leonardo DiCaprio. The door is wide open.

Motown music from a CD player. The window is open. A fly catches BARBIE-JEAN's eye: she frantically tries to make it go back out, wafting her hands at it, but to no avail; instead she accidentally kicks over a neat stack of books.

BARBIE-JEAN: Shit. (*Shouting.*) Jake! Jake! Come an' kill this fly will ya? I'm tryna do me 'air! (*She goes to the door.*) Jake! (*No answer.*)

She picks up the largest book and swats the fly on the dresser. She looks at the back of the book and sees the squashed insect.

Uurrgh!

She bangs the book on the window ledge so that the insect falls off and out. She puts the book down and closes the window.

Dead.

She tidies up the books and reads the cover of the one she used as a fly swat.

The Complete Works of Oscar Wilde. (*Talking to the book.*) Didn't expect that did ya?

She goes back over to the mirror and starts to paint her eyelashes. She goes out of the room and re-enters with some tissue paper, wiping it around her eyes. She begins to sing away to the music. Loud dance music suddenly bellows from the adjacent room. She goes to the door and screams.

Jake! Jake! Turn it down! (*No answer.*) Right.

She turns the volume up really high on her Motown track and starts dancing around, being careful not to knock things over. She opens the door and listens out. She turns off the CD. Silence. She goes back to painting her eyelashes. Practising her voice elocution in the mirror she sounds very posh. Her lips should be all over the place.

Rubber baby buggy bumper. Rubber baby buggy bumper.

Enter JAKE but she doesn't see him. He is 15 and looks like a walking billboard for sports brands – trainers, tracksuit, cap, and lots of gold jewellery.

Unique New York. Unique New York. Rubber baby buggy bumper. (*Suddenly catching JAKE out the corner of her eye.*) Rubber…

JAKE: (*Finishing off the sentence.*) Jonny. You're off ya 'ead you. Wha' are ya goin' on about?

BARBIE-JEAN: Get out spud 'ead!

JAKE: (*Laughing and falling back on BARBIE-JEAN's bed.*) I'm gonna tell all ya mates.

BARBIE-JEAN: At least I've got mates. I'm doin' me voice elocution ya divvie. Now get out!

JAKE: No ya freak.

BARBIE-JEAN: I've just tidied that bed. Get off it. And don't be comin' in 'ere with ya dirty trainers on – gettin' shit all over the carpet.

JAKE: Make me go then.

BARBIE-JEAN: You're disgustin'. You've weed all over the toilet seat.

JAKE: I 'aven't been for a wee. I went for a poo.

BARBIE-JEAN: There's wee everywhere.

JAKE: You can't talk.

BARBIE-JEAN: What do ya want?

JAKE: Everywhere ya go in this 'ouse it's covered in 'airs. It's like the soap's got a wig on it. Can't ya pick it... Eh, 'as me dad told ya about Auntie Pauline?

BARBIE-JEAN: No – wha'?

JAKE: She's comin' round soon. She's gotta big surprise apparently – for you.

BARBIE-JEAN: Go eh – what surprise?

JAKE: Dunno – 'e wouldn't say. Said 'e couldn't trust me not to tell ya. Wonder what it's about.

BARBIE-JEAN: What time's she comin'round?

JAKE: Don't ask me. Why?

BARBIE-JEAN: You know what it's all about don't ya?

JAKE: Don't be soft. 'E won't tell me nottin'. Look at the state o' your 'ead. Wha' 'ave you done to it?

BARBIE-JEAN: What do you want Jake? I'm busy.

JAKE: Looks like you've got pubic 'air growin' in the wrong place.

BARBIE-JEAN: Wha' would you know?

JAKE: (*Laughing.*) Fanny 'ead!

BARBIE-JEAN: Accordin' to a certain girl I know you 'aven't got any pubes, so there.

JAKE: (*Standing up.*) Ya lyin' bitch! She never said tha'. I 'ave got pubes!

Slight pause.

BARBIE-JEAN: Congratulations. Let's open the champagne shall we! Why don't ya go an' count them and then tell me 'ow many you've got? You've got a hairy arse an' that's about it. Now piss off.

JAKE: Can I borrow that tenner?

BARBIE-JEAN: No.

JAKE: Oh go on. Ahl arse.

BARBIE-JEAN: I 'aven't got any. Not to spare any way.

JAKE: Go way. Ya loaded. Birthday girl.

BARBIE-JEAN: What's it for?

JAKE: Wha' do ya think? It's the first night o' the summer 'olidies. Me and Tony are gettin' on to the birds in town.

BARBIE-JEAN: Don't think ya comin' to the 051…

Slight pause.

Come 'ere you.

JAKE: Wha'?

BARBIE-JEAN: Come 'ere I said.

JAKE: No. Why?

BARBIE-JEAN: Just come 'ere soft lad.

JAKE: No. Ya gonna…

BARBIE-JEAN: Do ya want that tenner or not?

JAKE: Yeh but…

BARBIE-JEAN: Come 'ere then!

Cautiously JAKE goes over. She sniffs his clothes.

You've been smokin' pot. Pot 'ead. I friggin' 'ate tha' smell. You dirty get.

JAKE: I 'aven't. Tony's dad was smokin' it round 'is 'ouse. I was there just now. 'Onest I 'aven't.

BARBIE-JEAN: You better get them clothes in the wash before 'e comes in. 'E'll be 'ome any minute. There'll be murder if 'e thinks…

JAKE: I 'aven't touched it.

BARBIE-JEAN: You know what 'e's like. Suspicion is conviction.

JAKE starts pulling off his tracksuit.

Not in 'ere divvie.

JAKE: 'E'll kill me. I'm in enough… Wha' if 'e smells it in the washin' basket?

BARBIE-JEAN: Not likely with your football kit in there. Giz 'em. I'll put 'em in 'ere.

JAKE: Thanks.

JAKE is now stripped down to a t-shirt and boxing shorts. BARBIE-JEAN shoves the tracksuit into the basket.

BARBIE-JEAN: 'E'll never look in there.

JAKE: Ya never know with 'im. Inspector Morse. 'E finds everything.

BARBIE-JEAN sprays the room with air freshener.

That stuff stinks.

BARBIE-JEAN: Better than your room. Smells like someone killed a cow in there.

JAKE: Slept with a few.

BARBIE-JEAN: Yeh right.

BARBIE-JEAN puts more spray on her hair.

JAKE: Can I borrow that tenner?

BARBIE-JEAN: No.

JAKE: Cow. I wouldn't put any more stuff on your 'air. It's already as stiff as a fuckin' poker. You'll end up breakin' someone's neck with it. Ya can't go out. 'E's grounded ya.

BARBIE-JEAN: That's wha' you think.

JAKE: You've been too long on that sun bed for a start anyway. You look terrible.

BARBIE-JEAN: It's not tha' ya divvie. It's just…

JAKE: Wha'?

BARBIE-JEAN: I shouldn't 'ave used the tan lotion *and* gone on the sun bed. Apparently. It makes ya skin go a bit funny.

JAKE: Ya tellin' me. You look like the curious orange. Who's gonna get off with you like tha'?

BARBIE-JEAN: Ya can't tell once I've put… I'm puttin' this special cream on. Ya won't be able to see it.

JAKE: You know when you've been tangoed.

BARBIE-JEAN: Shut up.

JAKE: No fella's gonna look at you in that state Barbie-Jean. Except to point and laugh.

BARBIE-JEAN: I'm warning you Jake. Get out! Or I'll tell me Dad…

JAKE: Ah shut it. Ya can't tell 'im anything 'cause you've been grounded, an' I know, tonight, right, you're gonna try an' sneak out, or, let me guess, I know, you'll go off to town an' tell 'im you've gone round to Stella's – (*Said very sarcastically.*) – studying. Is that it? Yeh later.

BARBIE-JEAN: Do I look as if I'm bothered?

JAKE: Later!

He grabs a makeup stick from BARBIE-JEAN's dresser.

BARBIE-JEAN: You better watch it lad!

He waves the make-up stick at her.

JAKE: Give us that tenner Barbie-Jean.

BARBIE-JEAN: Giz it back!

JAKE: Catch me.

BARBIE-JEAN: I'll scrag your little spud 'ead all round the
'ouse in a minute. Giz it back!

JAKE: Money first.

BARBIE-JEAN: Give us that lip gloss back or I'll break ya
bastard neck!

*She goes for him. There is a struggle. JAKE laughs as BARBIE-
JEAN pushes him onto the bed and tickles him. She gets the
lip gloss.*

Loser.

JAKE: You've still gotta give me the tenner – or I'll tell 'im
you're goin' out tonight.

BARBIE-JEAN: Like I'll tell 'im you're a pot 'ead.

JAKE: I'm not though.

BARBIE-JEAN: 'E'll still kick the shit out o' ya. Then I'll
give you a crack as well. Anyway, soft lad, I know
something you don't know.

JAKE: Yeh. Like wha'?

BARBIE-JEAN: It concerns you.

JAKE: (*Sitting up.*) Wha'?

BARBIE-JEAN: Wouldn't you like to know. Let's just say, a
little birdie told me your secret, an' if ya don't wan' 'im
to find out, you better watch it, or you 'll be dead.

*She gives him a big smile. Pause. BARBIE-JEAN goes back
to preening herself in the mirror.*

Make us a cup o' tea Jake. In fact, Stella's comin' round soon. Brew us a pot will ya? An' not your kinda pot neither.

JAKE: Alright clever arse tell us.

BARBIE-JEAN: No.

JAKE: 'Cause ya don't know nottin'.

BARBIE-JEAN: Wanna bet. Let's just say, I don't know why ya bothered to put your school uniform on all week, seein' as you weren't goin' to school.

JAKE: Where was I goin' then?

BARBIE-JEAN: Round to me nan an' grandad's. You've been suspended again.

JAKE: How do you know?

BARBIE-JEAN: Because nan told me stupid. She never said what for though. She just said don't let ya dad find out or 'e'll skin Jake alive.

JAKE: Does 'e know anythin'?

BARBIE-JEAN: Not yet.

JAKE: Wha' do ya mean, not yet?

BARBIE-JEAN: I mean if you don't stop pissin' around lad, if you don't get ya smelly carcass out o' my room, I might just let it slip.

JAKE: Me mum'll kill ya.

BARBIE-JEAN: Bit difficult at the moment, don't ya think?

JAKE: I'll tell 'im… I'll tell 'im – you'll be grounded all summer.

BARBIE-JEAN: Nottin's gonna stop me lad.

JAKE: Oh yer.

BARBIE-JEAN: Nottin's gonna stop me doin' wha' I wanna do.

JAKE: 'E will.

BARBIE-JEAN: Anyway wha' ever 'appens you're the one who'll get battered. I don't care. I don't care if 'e clobbers ya.

JAKE: Don't tell 'im Barbie-Jean.

BARBIE-JEAN: Wha' did ya do this time? Fightin' again?

BARBIE-JEAN is still making up her face.

JAKE: It wasn't me. Tony spat at some woolly back on the bus, comin' 'ome from school. I got dragged into the Head's office again didn't I? – just 'cause I 'ang round wid 'im. Ya won't tell me dad will ya?

BARBIE-JEAN: Promise then.

JAKE: Wha'?

BARBIE-JEAN: Promise you'll lie for me tonight, when 'e wants to know where I am.

JAKE: Alright. Give us a tenner.

BARBIE-JEAN: Deal.

She gives him the money out of an inside pocket. He examines the note.

I don't know. You've been actin' all funny ever since the' kicked you off tha' football team.

JAKE: I can still play for the school can't I?

BARBIE-JEAN: Not by the looks of it.

JAKE: I wasn't kicked off anyway.

BARBIE-JEAN: Yer right.

JAKE: Wha' do ya want me to say about tonight then?

BARBIE-JEAN: You know. I'm at Stella's, she's 'elpin' me…

The telephone rings. JAKE answers it.

JAKE: Hello. Alright. I'll just get 'er. (*To BARBIE-JEAN.*) Barbie-Jean; it's mum. She wants to speak to ya.

BARBIE-JEAN: Tell 'er I'm dead.

JAKE: (*Covering the receiver.*) Speak to 'er Barbie-Jean.

BARBIE-JEAN goes to the telephone and takes it off JAKE.

BARBIE-JEAN: Hello – mum. Yeh listen – piss off!

She slams the receiver down and goes back to the mirror.

JAKE: You're out of order!

BARBIE-JEAN: Get stuffed!

JAKE: You shouldn't… It's not me mother's fault.

BARBIE-JEAN: I don't care!

JAKE: I don't know why…

Slight pause.

Turn round Barbie-Jean.

BARBIE-JEAN: Wha'?

JAKE: Just turn round.

She does so.

Oh my God! Wha' 'ave you done?

BARBIE-JEAN: Why? Do de look dead fake?

BARBIE-JEAN flutters her eyelashes in demonstration.

JAKE: They look like spiders' legs.

BARBIE-JEAN: They won't fall off. They're glued on.

JAKE: Let's feel.

JAKE touches BARBIE-JEAN's eyelashes.

'Eee. They feel dead funny.

She goes back to slapping on the makeup.

What's 'e gonna 'ave to say about that?

BARBIE-JEAN: 'E won't notice.

JAKE: Bet 'e does. 'E will ya know.

BARBIE-JEAN: It's not 'is money is it?

JAKE: 'Ow much did it cost?

BARBIE-JEAN: Forty quid.

JAKE: Forty quid for a pair o' fake eyelashes! Goay! I could o' got more realistic ones out of a Christmas cracker.

BARBIE-JEAN: Don't say that. Can ya really tell?

JAKE: I bet ya psycho'll make you take 'em off.

BARBIE-JEAN: They're glued on. They need to be surgically removed.

JAKE: That won't stop 'im. Shit!

BARBIE-JEAN: Wha'?

JAKE: 'Is van's outside.

BARBIE-JEAN: Did you 'ear the door open?

JAKE: No. I don't know.

BARBIE-JEAN: Shit!

She frantically rummages through a draw. JAKE goes to leave, but KEVIN pushes him back into the room as he enters. He is aged 45 and still in his work dungarees. He is also wearing plastic gloves.

KEVIN: What's goin' on in 'ere?

He tortures JAKE in a playful, routine form.

JAKE: Ow! Get off dad!

KEVIN: Don't forget where the pressure points are Jake.

JAKE yelps as KEVIN pokes various parts of his body, the father laughing as his son falls helplessly to the floor.

Wha' are ya doin' walkin' round the 'ouse wid no clothes on? Eh?

JAKE: Nottin'.

KEVIN: Wha'?

He pokes him again. JAKE screams.

Wha' I said?

JAKE: I was just gettin' changed.

KEVIN: Get up then.

JAKE gets up.

Walkin' round the 'ouse like a fuckin' savage. This is a civilised family unit.

He attacks JAKE again, this time making mock, karate-chop noises. JAKE is backed off into a corner.

Come on son!

JAKE: Get off!

KEVIN laughs.

Alright we all know you've got ya black belt.

KEVIN: Great isn't it. The only thing you'll ever get a black belt in is being fucking useless.

KEVIN laughs and notices BARBIE-JEAN. She is wearing a ridiculous pair of pink sunglasses.

Fuckin' 'ell. An' they said Timmy Mallett would never make a comeback.

BARBIE-JEAN: What's all this about Auntie Pauline?

JAKE goes to leave.

KEVIN: Don't be tryin' to escape you.

KEVIN gets JAKE in a headlock and pulls him down as he sits on BARBIE-JEAN's bed.

JAKE: Get off dad!

KEVIN: Where does my lovely boy think 'e's goin' without 'is daddy?

He gives him a bear hug.

JAKE: Ow – that 'urts dad.

KEVIN: Arh – my little boy. It's meant to 'urt, you ungrateful bastard. I 'ope you've been a good lad at school for me eh? If I find out there's been any trouble, there'll be murder.

JAKE: No dad.

KEVIN: Don't forget, you're comin' to work with me tomorra.

He ruffles his head then lets him go.

JAKE: Don't remind me.

BARBIE-JEAN: Come on dad – what's the big surprise then?

KEVIN: (*To JAKE.*) Set ya alarm for six. (*To BARBIE-JEAN.*) Get them sunglasses off. You look fuckin' stupid. Wearin' sunglasses indoors. Who do you think you are – Michael fucking Jackson?

BARBIE-JEAN: Says a man wearin' plastic gloves.

KEVIN: I 'ave to wear these stupid. It's called 'avin' a fuckin' job. Argh. Fuckin' threw up in the fuckin' pub last night didn't I? Must o' been that pasta shit ya gave me.

BARBIE-JEAN: As if six pints o' lager an' a bottle o' wine 'ad nottin' to do with it.

KEVIN: I'm tellin' ya. It was that pasta. 'Ave you been on tha' sunbed again? Stay off it – you already look like Tutankhamun.

BARBIE-JEAN: Are ya gonna tell us then or not?

KEVIN: Wha' about?

BARBIE-JEAN: You know wha'. What's the big surprise?

KEVIN: Don't know wha' ya mean.

BARBIE-JEAN: Auntie Pauline's gotta big surprise Jake said, for me.

KEVIN: Oh yeh. I don't know wha' you're getting all dolled up for. Ya not goin' anywhere. That's for certain.

BARBIE-JEAN: Stella's comin' round.

JAKE: Posh bitch.

KEVIN smacks JAKE over the head.

KEVIN: Don't talk about Stella like that.

BARBIE-JEAN: What's it all about then?

KEVIN: You'll find out when Pauline gets 'ere.

BARBIE-JEAN: When will that be? She's gotta come all the way from Rhyl 'asn't she? She could be ages.

KEVIN: It's only an hour on the train. I thought she might be 'ere by now.

BARBIE-JEAN: Well she's not. So tell me.

KEVIN: Jake, put the kettle on bud.

JAKE: I'm talkin' to youse.

BARBIE-JEAN: God!

KEVIN: You can talk an' make tea at the same time. An' while ya down there wash the dishes.

JAKE huffs as he goes.

Get your arse down there.

BARBIE-JEAN: No sugar for me Jake.

JAKE exits.

Dad just tell me an' stop teasin'!

KEVIN: No – you'll find out when she arrives. Can't be long now.

BARBIE-JEAN: I 'ate you.

KEVIN: You kids can't wait for anything.

BARBIE-JEAN: Give us a clue.

KEVIN: 'E are what's this, four words? I'm tellin' ya nottin' – shut ya wingin' gob. That's final. 'As ya mum phoned?

BARBIE-JEAN: No.

KEVIN: Good. If I find 'er family's been round 'ere, I'm tellin' ya – no-one, if any o' them bastards…

BARBIE-JEAN: The' won't dad.

KEVIN: They started all this. Poisonin' 'er fuckin' mind.

BARBIE-JEAN: It's alright if Stella comes round though, isn't it?

KEVIN: Where is she now?

BARBIE-JEAN: Who – Stella?

KEVIN: No divvie ya mum.

BARBIE-JEAN: I don't know.

KEVIN: Yes you do.

BARBIE-JEAN: I won't speak… She's still at me nan's.

KEVIN: Typical. I'll be the flavour o' the fuckin' month round there then, as usual.

BARBIE-JEAN: What flavour's that do you think?

KEVIN: If she wants to stay in fuckin' Speke all 'er life, that's up to 'er. (*BARBIE-JEAN sighs; she has heard all this before.*) I offer to buy 'er a nice 'ouse in Aigburth, lovely garden, the lot. On no. (*In a mocking tone.*) 'I wanna be near me family.' Fuck off.

BARBIE-JEAN: She might o' still been 'ere now, if you 'adn't kept puttin' pressure on 'er. Ya know what she's like.

KEVIN: (*Laughing.*) Yeh.

BARBIE-JEAN: An' it didn't 'elp much bannin' all 'er family from comin' round, did it?

KEVIN: Eh…eh, eh, eh.

The telephone rings. BARBIE-JEAN answers it.

BARBIE-JEAN: Alright Stella. Yeh. I can't talk to ya right now.

KEVIN: Yes ya can.

BARBIE-JEAN: Wha'? Why not? I can't. Just come round first, I need to speak to ya. Come round.

She puts down the receiver.

KEVIN: Wha' are you up to?

BARBIE-JEAN: Nottin'.

She sprays the room with air freshener again, particularly near the basket.

KEVIN: Wha' are ya doin'? Tryna say I smell?

BARBIE-JEAN: Yes.

JAKE re-enters with two mugs of tea and then exits.

KEVIN: (*To BARBIE-JEAN.*) 'Ow are the A-Levels getting on? What's this play again, you're suppose to be studyin'?

BARBIE-JEAN: Lady Fandemere's Wind.

KEVIN: Wha'?

BARBIE-JEAN: *Lady Windermere's Fan.* Or something. It's a bit borin' really. All these stuffy old people sittin' around talkin' rubbish.

KEVIN: Sounds like a night down at The Fox. Come on – let's see wha' notes you've made.

BARBIE-JEAN: I don't need to make notes.

KEVIN: Don't lie. You told me last Sunday you were gonna sit down an' make notes on each character in the play.

BARBIE-JEAN: I've done that.

KEVIN: Let's see then.

BARBIE-JEAN: Don't be stupid. What do you wanna see me notes for? You won't understand them.

KEVIN: I understand enough… I know enough to know when you're not pullin' your weight girl.

BARBIE-JEAN hands him her note book.

BARBIE-JEAN: 'Ere.

KEVIN: Tar. (*Starting to look through.*)

BARBIE-JEAN: It's not marked or nottin' you know. Mr Broadbent 'asn't got time for lookin' at note books, 'e said. 'E just wants the essays. 'E 'as to look after 'is wife on the weekends.

KEVIN: What's up with 'er?

31

BARBIE-JEAN: She's dead big, apparently.

KEVIN: Where's ya character notes then?

BARBIE-JEAN: 'Ere

She shows him.

KEVIN: Is tha' it?

BARBIE-JEAN: Yeh.

KEVIN: That's all you've done? Ya takin' piss aren't ya girl – a scrawled sentence for each character. My fuckin' signature's longer than this. Where's this gonna get ya?

BARBIE-JEAN: Ya don't know nottin' do ya?

KEVIN: Don't I? Tell me then.

BARBIE-JEAN: Wha'?

KEVIN: Tell me wha' I don't know.

BARBIE-JEAN: I 'aven't got all year.

KEVIN: Very funny. Dead clever you aren't ya? Could fit on a stamp what you don't know. Anyway you've got more time than me 'cause I've grounded ya till I see more work getting done. (*He laughs.*)

BARBIE-JEAN: Look, basically, well…

KEVIN: Yeh, go on.

BARBIE-JEAN: Erm, well, right, in Oscar Wilde's plays, right, the characters are basically… There's not much to them. They're two-dimensional, is what I'm tryna say. They 'aven't got much depth – they're more a vehicle for Wilde's subversive epigrams and paradoxical wit. Put another way, there's not much to say about them as psychologically consistent characters, as there might be for example in a play by Ibsen or Chekhov.

Slight pause.

KEVIN: Barbie.

BARBIE-JEAN: Yeh?

KEVIN: You memorised all that.

BARBIE-JEAN: So.

KEVIN: Ya sound like ya readin' from a fuckin' autocue; is Mr Broadbent outside? What does paradoxical mean then? Isn't tha' when a tart dyes her hair blonde?

BARBIE-JEAN: I don't know what it means. I don't know – something about a statement being contradictory but true. 'Ow the hell should I know?

KEVIN: Because you're meant be studyin' the fuckin' thing. Ya suppose to know about the Queen's English, aren't ya?

BARBIE-JEAN: Oscar Wilde wasn't English.

KEVIN: 'E was a fuckin' queen though. I know that much.

BARBIE-JEAN: What do you expect – 'e was a writer. It's an occupational hazard; a bit like you getting knobbly knees from fittin' gas fires all day.

KEVIN: So basically you've done fuck all work.

BARBIE-JEAN: I 'ave. I've done me essay. There's no point in makin' loads o' notes.

KEVIN: 'Ow are ya suppose to revise then soft girl?

BARBIE-JEAN: It's called reading the text.

KEVIN: Yeh. Text messages more like, between you an' Miss United fucking Kingdom.

BARBIE-JEAN: Who?

KEVIN: Stella. (*Sipping his tea.*)

BARBIE-JEAN: Look, I've done something, 'aven't I? Can I go out?

KEVIN: No.

BARBIE-JEAN: Why not?

KEVIN: Because I said.

BARBIE-JEAN: God. Stella does nothing and she goes out whenever she likes.

KEVIN: That's 'er business. I want you to get an education.

BARBIE-JEAN: I am doin'. What do you think me A-Levels are all about? I'm not doin' it for fun you know.

KEVIN: There's no point moanin'. The only thing that's gonna make any difference to me, the only thing, right, that's gonna persuade me to let you out anywhere – is evidence of some proper studyin' bein' done.

BARBIE-JEAN: I've been workin' 'ard all week.

KEVIN: Evidence, I said. I wan' evidence.

BARBIE-JEAN: An' who are you all of a sudden – Rumpole o' Bailey?

KEVIN: Ya can talk the talk girl – it means nottin' to me. I wanna see some stuff written down on paper.

BARBIE-JEAN: One night's not gonna make any difference. Why are ya bein' dead mean all of a sudden?

KEVIN: I'm not bein' dead mean. It's not all of a sudden either. I warned you weeks ago. I said to ya, get some proper work done – before the summer 'oliday starts, then ya can just enjoy yourself. But ya won't listen will ya. Look at ya now.

BARBIE-JEAN: Wha'?

KEVIN: Dollin' yourself up in the mirror like some great big fuckin' film actress, without a film.

Enter STELLA; same age as BARBIE-JEAN. She is average in height, build and appearance and has dyed blonde hair.

She is wearing a 'slash-neck' top and is dressed for a night out: her speech has no accent.

STELLA: Sorry. The front door was open.

KEVIN: Workin' 'ard then Stella?

STELLA: Yes thanks.

KEVIN: Good.

KEVIN exits.

STELLA: How's the voice elocution going?

BARBIE-JEAN: Not bad.

STELLA: (*Sarcastically.*) Sounds it.

BARBIE-JEAN: Piss off. You watch; I'll get there.

BARBIE-JEAN takes the sunglasses off.

STELLA: What are you wearing those for? What's going on?

BARBIE-JEAN: Me dad's bein' an absolute bastard again.

STELLA: Call the police.

BARBIE-JEAN: Ya jokin' aren't ya? We need Amnesty International when 'e kicks off.

STELLA: My dad's not like that with me.

BARBIE-JEAN: That's different.

STELLA: Is it? Oh yeah, sorry. I forgot about your mum not being here.

BARBIE-JEAN: No. I mean – your dad not being your real dad.

STELLA: (*Sighs.*) You're not going to start that again are you?

BARBIE-JEAN: I didn't say anything.

35

STELLA: It's obviously more of a problem for you than it is for me.

BARBIE-JEAN: I didn't mean that.

STELLA: Stop going on about it.

BARBIE-JEAN: Sorry.

Slight pause.

STELLA: So why did I have to come round here? Speke is like such a dump. Why couldn't we just meet up in town?

BARBIE-JEAN: I might need ya 'elp.

STELLA: (*Inspecting BARBIE-JEAN's makeup collection.*) What for?

BARBIE-JEAN: Getting out o' this place. 'E won't let me go anywhere.

STELLA: Barbie – you knew you were grounded anyway. I thought you were going to sneak out.

BARBIE-JEAN: I might 'ave to.

STELLA: You just don't like the idea of me having a good time without you. You'd rather I was stuck in doors with you.

BARBIE-JEAN: That's not true.

STELLA: Or it's more complicated than that.

BARBIE-JEAN: It is from my angle.

STELLA: What?

BARBIE-JEAN: Look, my Auntie Pauline's coming round any minute now.

STELLA: Oh God she's not coming with us.

BARBIE-JEAN: Not necessarily.

STELLA: What does that mean – not necessarily?

BARBIE-JEAN: It might be the only way. She's gotta big surprise for me apparently.

STELLA: What – she can actually get to the end of a sentence without saying 'fuck'?

BARBIE-JEAN: I don't know what the surprise is. Me dad won't tell me. I'm dyin' to find out.

STELLA: (*Sarcastically.*) Can't wait. It's probably a really cheap piece of jewellery she's got you from a fairground; I bet you she thinks it's just like so gorgeous. You'll just smile and agree as always: 'Thank you Auntie Pauline'.

BARBIE-JEAN: The point is, if Pauline comes with us, me dad might let me go out.

STELLA: Great. That's really going to make the boys want to talk to us isn't it, being seen with her? I want more than talk tonight.

BARBIE-JEAN: She might even persuade him to let us go out on our own. She has that kind o' power over 'im. It's a woman thing.

STELLA: More like he's frightened she'll belt him one.

BARBIE-JEAN: There is that.

STELLA: I'm not staying in with you if you can't go out.

BARBIE-JEAN: Don't say that. I've got to go out 'aven't I? You know.

STELLA: Thought as much. (*Going over to her.*) Look, Barbie, I know you don't believe me, won't believe me, listen, I don't fancy Mark, okay? It's not as if like I'm going to get off with him, even if you're not there. I wouldn't even try. I know what I want: just give me a man who's tall, dark and handsome, mid to late twenties, absolutely rolling in cash; and that's not Mark now is it?

I know you think that every boy you fancy is like universally gorgeous…

BARBIE-JEAN: If you don't cop off with 'im someone else might.

STELLA: It's not as if you've got anything going with him – yet.

BARBIE-JEAN: Exactly, that's just it. If I don't turn up tonight some other girl might get 'im. God I think 'e's like just so…arrh; look, I told 'im I'd meet up with 'im tonight, if I don't turn up…

STELLA: I told him. Don't forget I set you up with him, like I always have to. You're too bloody shy.

BARBIE-JEAN: I've got to meet 'im tonight Stella. I wanna be with 'im.

STELLA: What happens if you can't go out?

BARBIE-JEAN: I've told you, don't even say that.

STELLA: Your dad won't budge.

BARBIE-JEAN: I'm workin' on it.

STELLA: It's best if I go even if you don't. That way I can make sure Mark doesn't cop off…

BARBIE-JEAN: Look, Stella, I've to get to that club tonight if the last thing I ever do. Stop being so…fatalistic. You're not the Oracle of Delphi. Are ya gonna try an' 'elp me or not?

STELLA: What can I do?

BARBIE-JEAN: I'm goin' out to see Mark an' that's final.

STELLA: What about your dad?

BARBIE-JEAN: I'll just go out when e's not lookin', if I 'ave to.

Offstage KEVIN is heard screaming at JAKE – 'Get tha' fuckin' dog in the back yard'.

BARBIE-JEAN goes to the window. Enter KEVIN, PAULINE and JAKE. She is 40 years old, about fifteen stone and is wearing tight cotton pants that only come up to her knees. She is out of breath and carrying one small bag.

PAULINE: Fuckin' late again. Got off at Lime Street didn't I? – went shoppin' in town.

BARBIE-JEAN: What's the big surprise?

PAULINE: I nearly stood in shit comin' up that path.

KEVIN: It's tha' fuckin' dog of 'is. Max.

PAULINE: Mad Max.

JAKE: Our dog.

KEVIN: I'm getting it put down.

JAKE: Ya not dad.

PAULINE: Make sure it doesn't get in me shoppin' bags. Oh eh I'm shattered.

JAKE: At least our dog doesn't bite people.

KEVIN: No. It just tries to shag them.

JAKE: Only strange men.

PAULINE: I know 'ow it feels.

KEVIN: It's gotta thing for Jake's mates.

JAKE: I know. It's been up Tony's leg God knows 'ow many times. 'E's only fourteen.

KEVIN: Who – the dog?

JAKE: No. Tony.

KEVIN: Only fourteen. It's a case for Esther Rantzen, isn't it?

39

PAULINE: It 'ud 'ave a fuckin' job tryna shag me. More chance o' climbin' Mount Everest. Get me a chair Jake. I wanna try me new slippers on.

JAKE gets her a chair. She sits down.

BARBIE-JEAN: Are ya gonna tell us the surprise then?

PAULINE puts on her slippers; they are the type with bunny-rabbit heads.

PAULINE: In a minute. Ya won't believe it. I'm puttin' me bags on the Hunts Cross train, ya know, I lift them on first; next minute, the doors start closin' – I'm standin' on the platform thinkin', I'll never see me new knickers again. Anyway, I finally get on the train like, the guard comes down the platform. I'm by the door goin', eh you ya fuckin' knob; wha' the fuck are ya doin' ya dickhead? Fuckin' tryna ge' me bags on the train 'ere – closin' the doors on me! 'E went to me, it just looked as if you were standin' there, lookin' at the train. I went, 'ow the fuck do ya work tha' one out? Fuckin' tosser. They're all sittin' there lookin' at me on the train. I went, wha' the fuck are you lot like? Then 'e gave me the wrong fuckin' ticket. I wouldn't mind only it only ever goes the same place. 'Ow are you then Barbie love? All dolled up an' nowhere to go?

BARBIE-JEAN: I know.

BARBIE-JEAN gives KEVIN a resentful look.

PAULINE: We'll soon fix that.

BARBIE-JEAN: (*To STELLA, smiling.*) Sounds good.

PAULINE: 'Ow are you Stella babe?

STELLA: Fine thanks Pauline.

PAULINE: You look dead nice.

STELLA: Thank you.

KEVIN: Tell these about our John.

PAULINE: Don't get me started. Kevin, you're gonna 'ave to come back up with us tonight, an' sought 'im out.

KEVIN: I can't lovely. I've got work on. Ring the police.

PAULINE: They're fuckin' useless.

KEVIN: We don't even know where 'e is.

PAULINE: I know but – it's best if you're there in case 'e comes round again.

KEVIN: Pauline, I can't run up to Wales every time 'e's on the rampage. For a start, wha' are ya gonna do when I'm not there?

PAULINE: Ya never are. Last time 'e smashed the window tryna ge' in. I 'ad to run into the back yard – came back, found 'im lyin' on the carpet with 'is arms covered in blood. 'E's fuckin' mental.

KEVIN: 'E's an alcoholic. That's all there is to it.

PAULINE: 'E's your brother.

KEVIN: You fuckin' married 'im.

PAULINE: I know. I blame you. You introduced us. You got me pissed enough to say yes at the wedding – some fuckin' wedding tha' was.

KEVIN: I thought 'e was in a unit.

STELLA: What – like a mental hospital?

BARBIE-JEAN: No. For alcoholics.

PAULINE: 'E's been out two months now. Come on Kevin come up – just until, you know, the big day.

BARBIE-JEAN: Wha' big day?

JAKE: Yeh; tell us what's goin' on.

KEVIN: No. I can't. I'd lose too much business.

PAULINE: You'd come if our Angie was 'ere.

KEVIN: She's not though is she?

BARBIE-JEAN: Where ya goin'?

KEVIN: Go straight from 'ere.

PAULINE: No. We need to be back at my place tonight. All me stuff's there.

BARBIE-JEAN: What's goin' on?

PAULINE: The police station 'ave got me mobile number just in case – I tell ya, if 'e gets in my way this time, if 'e ends up in 'ospital again, I don't care what 'appens to 'im. I'm goin'.

JAKE: Goin' where?

PAULINE: 'E's just a greedy piss 'ead. 'E's mingin'; 'e smells an' everything. 'E's in an' out of 'ospital, this, that an' the other, 'e gets fuckin' battered to fuck – I rang you didn't I, I said, oh, I think 'e's nearly dead, e's in 'ospital. 'E's 'ad the shit kicked out of 'im I don't know 'ow many times. I just wan' 'im to fuckin' drop dead. All tha' just for ale. 'E's all over the place – wid all kinds. Anyone who'll get pissed an' put up with 'im. 'E just uses people. 'Ow many times 'as 'e robbed my 'ouse?

KEVIN: I've told ya time an' time again – ge' an injunction order.

PAULINE: 'E's been done for shop liftin'. 'E always gets away with it.

STELLA: How come?

PAULINE: 'E's classified an alcoholic. Four times 'e's fucked off with a trolley full o' booze. Our Kerry keeps goin' – who's gonna pay for 'is fuckin' funeral? She won't be outta pocket. I said, the soshe'll pay for it. Just go down the soshe an' say me dad's dead – 'ave ya got any money? They'll give you a thousand pounds an' say – 'e are, bury 'im.

BARBIE-JEAN: What's the surprise Auntie Pauline? 'Cause if it's about uncle John…

PAULINE: No – listen – I need to sit down for this. I might fall over with excitement.

JAKE pulls her a chair. She sits down.

Eh – get us a drink lad?

JAKE: Wha'?

PAULINE: Any orange juice?

JAKE: No.

KEVIN: Some lagers in the fridge.

PAULINE: Bit early for that. I 'ave to watch me figure.

JAKE: We've got pop.

PAULINE: That'll do.

JAKE fetches the drink.

BARBIE-JEAN: Go on.

PAULINE: Wha'?

BARBIE-JEAN: Tell us. Tell us the surprise.

PAULINE: It depends on uncle John.

BARBIE-JEAN: I thought it 'ad nottin' to do with…

PAULINE: It 'asn't. No' really. It's just – if 'e 'ends up… I might 'ave to cancel. Someone's gotta be there.

BARBIE-JEAN: Cancel what?

JAKE returns with a glass of lemonade. He hands it to PAULINE.

43

PAULINE: Tar love.

She drinks it. They all stand round her waiting for the announcement.

BARBIE-JEAN: Pauline tell us!

PAULINE: Alright. Remember me *Daily Express* coupons?

JAKE: Wha'?

PAULINE: The 'oliday coupons I got from the *Daily Express*. I won it didn't I? Fate fuckin' shines on me at last. I've won an 'oliday.

JAKE: Where to?

BARBIE-JEAN: When?

PAULINE: I 'ad a choice o' four destinations. Let's think know: 'ere – somewhere in Yorkshire – Bridlington; Wales – obviously no; somewhere in Norfolk – couldn't imagine much goin' on there – no fuck in Norfolk, an', o' course, Torquay. So I chose…

JAKE: Torquay?

PAULINE: Is right. A caravan 'oliday in Torquay. For a whole week.

Slight pause. She looks round.

Don't all fuckin' congratulate me at once.

JAKE: Great.

STELLA: Torquay's nice.

JAKE: 'Ave you ever been?

STELLA: No.

PAULINE: I know I'm easily excited but, fuckin' 'ell, we don't 'ave to start raisin' the dead. Cheer up ya miserable bastards.

BARBIE-JEAN: Are Kerry an' the baby goin'?

PAULINE: Oh yeh right; an' 'er fella – 'giz a job' – you think I'd take 'im on 'oliday wid me?

BARBIE-JEAN: You goin' on ya own?

PAULINE: No.

JAKE: No?

PAULINE: No.

BARBIE-JEAN: Who are ya goin' wid then?

PAULINE: Well – as I'll be on the look out for 'andsome young men, it might be an idea to bring an extra female with me. For safety.

JAKE: Who?

PAULINE: Are you free tonight Barbie-Jean?

BARBIE-JEAN: (*Looking at STELLA, horrified.*) Me?

PAULINE: Yeh. Don't worry. Ya dad's already promised to let me take ya. 'E can't change 'is mind. We're gonna go back to my place tonight and then get the train from Rhyl, first thing in the mornin'. It leaves dead early.

KEVIN: (*To BARBIE-JEAN.*) Now ya know why I wanted ya to get all ya work done – out the way, before ya go away; instead, you'll 'ave to do it all when you come back now, won't ya? It's a good job ya didn't plan to go out tonight isn't it?

JAKE: Wha' about me?

BARBIE-JEAN: Tonight?

PAULINE: Ge' packin'.

JAKE: Why can't I go?

PAULINE: You're too young.

JAKE: I'm not! I've seen more action than our Barbie any day.

JAKE exits.

PAULINE: Who's 'e kiddin'? We'll 'ave to leave straight after tea. Don't forget – this time o' year, Torquay's full…

BARBIE-JEAN: (*Looking at STELLA.*) I can't go!

PAULINE: Wha'?

KEVIN: Wha' do ya mean – can't?

STELLA: Why not?

BARBIE-JEAN: (*To KEVIN.*) Well, I've got all me work to do, 'aven't I?

KEVIN: You'll do all that when you get back. Believe me. Ya still grounded.

PAULINE: What's this about bein' grounded?

BARBIE-JEAN looks at KEVIN.

Stop 'avin' a go at 'er all the time you miserable cunt!

KEVIN: You don't know wha' goes on in this 'ouse.

PAULINE: I sometimes wonder.

KEVIN: I'm tryna make 'er ge' an education aren't I?

PAULINE: Just give 'er a fuckin' break from time to time!

KEVIN: She's goin' on 'olidee isn't she, doesn't that count as a break? It's more than I'm getting.

KEVIN exits.

STELLA: God I wish I could go.

PAULINE: Ya can.

STELLA: Can I?

BARBIE-JEAN nods at STELLA as if to say 'no'.

PAULINE: Don't see why not. Plenty o' room. I just wanna keep it a girls' thing. (*Winking at STELLA.*) Know what I mean?

STELLA: I think so. Oh Barbie we'll have such a laugh.

BARBIE-JEAN: (*Angrily.*) Wha' are ya sayin'?

STELLA: Are you sure Jake isn't going? I mean I don't want to take anyone's place.

PAULINE: Told ya – girls only. Anyway you'd better ask your mum first 'adn't ya?

STELLA: Oh yeh.

PAULINE: (*To BARBIE-JEAN.*) What's the long face for? Don't ya wanna go on 'oliday?

STELLA: I'll just give my mum a ring.

PAULINE: Tell 'er you'll need loads o' money.

STELLA: I will. (*Sensing the atmosphere.*) I'll use the downstairs phone.

STELLA exits.

PAULINE: Well then. What's ya problem? There's no point in stayin' 'ere – 'e's grounded ya.

Slight pause.

Is it our Angie – is it ya mum?

BARBIE-JEAN: (*Standing.*) No – look. Me an' Stella, we've got this big night planned – tonight. I was gonna try an' sneak out.

PAULINE: You'll 'ave a job with 'im won't ya?

BARBIE-JEAN: There's this dead fit lad I met last week in '051' – 'is name's Mark. We've arranged to meet 'im tonight – you see, if I go back to Wales with you now – an' then a week in Toquay, I'll miss the chance of a lifetime Auntie Pauline.

PAULINE: Don't talk soft!

BARBIE-JEAN: You 'aven't seen 'im. God 'e's gorgeous. I really like 'im.

PAULINE: An' wha' if you stay an' find you can't ge' out – wha' if 'e locks you in the fuckin' room or something? You know 'e's fuckin' mental. They all are. I should know. I married 'is fuckin' brother.

BARBIE-JEAN: If I'm there tonight I'm in with a good chance.

PAULINE: Yis need a break from each other. Give ya dad some space.

BARBIE-JEAN: I mean 'e's expectin' me, isn't 'e?

PAULINE: 'E's been under a lot o' pressure 'imself really, wha' with Angie leavin' 'im. Still, no excuse for takin' it out on you.

BARBIE-JEAN: Oh God wha' am I gonna do? Why does everything 'ave to be so difficult?

PAULINE: Exactly. I mean if 'e's grounded ya – wha' next? 'E'll 'ave ya chained to the fuckin' floor before ya know it. You've gotta ge' away from 'im.

BARBIE-JEAN: Wha' about Mark?

PAULINE: 'Ave ya got 'is mobile number, I mean this Mark lad?

BARBIE-JEAN: No, but 'e's got mine.

PAULINE: 'E'll still be in Liverpool when you get back.

BARBIE-JEAN: It's not the point. 'E'll 'ave found some other girl by then – an' if – it's not worth thinkin' about. (*Almost crying.*) Don't ya see!

PAULINE: There'll be plenty o' chances.

BARBIE-JEAN: Auntie Pauline ya don't understand. I can't stop thinkin' about 'im. I'm in love!

PAULINE: Shut ya wingin' gob. Shut ya gob an' listen to me. Sit down.

BARBIE-JEAN sits. KEVIN enters.

This is women's talk.

KEVIN: I 'ope she's not tellin' lies…

PAULINE: Nottin' to do with you ahl arse. Just fuck off out of it. Close the door after ya.

KEVIN exits, closing the door tight.

Listen girl – I understand about fellas alright. Believe me, there's plenty more where this one came from, by the sounds of it…

BARBIE-JEAN: If only you'd seen 'im. 'E's the cutest lad in the world. If 'e's found another girlfriend by the time I get back…

PAULINE: 'E's obviously a twat then isn't 'e – if 'e's not prepared to wait. Anyway, if 'e's that gorgeous, then 'e's more trouble than 'e's worth – believe me. You'd 'ave to keep ya eye on 'im all the time. If 'e doesn't break ya 'eart – then it'll be ya fuckin' purse – at least.

BARBIE-JEAN sobs.

Come 'ere. Come an' sit next to ya Auntie Pauline.

BARBIE-JEAN sits next to PAULINE on the bed.

Anyway – don't ya know, this time o' year, Torquay's full o' fit lads on 'oliday, mostly from Liverpool. So if ya met someone, chances are, you could keep in touch.

BARBIE-JEAN: Really?

PAULINE: Yeh. Why do ya think I chose Torquay? It's full o' gorgeous lads. In the summer the' all walk round wid no clothes on, an' lovely golden tans – like yours.

BARBIE-JEAN: Are you serious?

PAULINE: Very serious. Tell you a little secret, I'm actually after some fella; this dead posh bloke, a teacher – but 'e's alright. Works at a private school – I used to be a cleaner there, many years ago, when I lived in Torquay. Let's just say, 'is desk wasn't the only thing I polished.

Enter STELLA.

STELLA: Mum's gone the bingo.

PAULINE: Ah aye. That's a shame.

STELLA: It's alright. I persuaded my dad. He said I can go.

PAULINE: Sound.

STELLA: Come on Barbie. Are you happy now?

BARBIE-JEAN: Dead 'appy.

They hug each other.

STELLA: It'll be so cool.

BARBIE-JEAN: You're not goin' anywhere tonight then?

STELLA: No way. I'm coming with you.

BARBIE-JEAN: Auntie Pauline, tell Stella about all the fit lads in Torquay.

PAULINE: The caravan site's walkin' distance from the beach, so I'm told. We'll be right near the night clubs as well, where all the lads are.

STELLA: I just so can't wait to get down there.

Enter JAKE.

JAKE: (*To PAULINE.*) If I came I could go fishin'.

50

BARBIE-JEAN: No way.

PAULINE: Anyway ya can't now. Stella's comin'. There'll be no room.

BARBIE-JEAN: It's just us girls. No boys, thank you very much.

JAKE: Shut up.

BARBIE-JEAN: You'll just 'ave to stay 'ere with me dad – you and ya smelly fishing tackle.

PAULINE: Stella, tell ya dad we'll be goin' straight after tea.

BARBIE-JEAN: (*To STELLA.*) 'Ave tea with us.

STELLA: Are you sure your dad won't mind?

PAULINE: I said ya can.

BARBIE-JEAN: I'm cookin' it.

STELLA: Oh this is so cool.

BARBIE-JEAN and STELLA kiss each other and laugh.

JAKE: Eeee, ge' away ya lesbians.

PAULINE: Settled then. (*Standing up.*) We're goin' on 'oliday. We're off to Torquay! Fuck off Speke!

She makes a two fingered gesture out of the window.

Say fuck off Speke. Fuckin' piss 'ole.

BARBIE-JEAN: Fuck off Speke!

JAKE: Shut up Barbie.

PAULINE: Say fuck off dad!

BARBIE-JEAN: (*Just as KEVIN enters the room.*) Fuck off dad!

Slight pause.

KEVIN: What's goin' on?

PAULINE: Ah shut up you. 'Cause we're goin' on 'oliday, an' you're fuckin' not! (*She laughs.*) Tell 'im to fuck off! (*She laughs again.*) By the way Stella's 'avin' tea with us.

Exit JAKE.

STELLA: If it's okay.

KEVIN: I'll be glad to be shut o' yis.

BARBIE-JEAN: I've just remembered – this means I don't 'ave to do any revision next week. Yesss!

PAULINE: Say fuck off revision – hello boys!

KEVIN: Alright Judith Chalmers. Calm down will ya.

PAULINE: Let's open tha' fuckin' lager.

KEVIN: You've gotta watch 'er ya know. It'll be spend, spend, spend if ya not careful.

PAULINE: You'll 'ave to give 'er some money.

KEVIN: Jokin' aren't ya?

BARBIE-JEAN: Auntie Pauline – come an' see me new bath salts.

KEVIN, PAULINE and BARBIE-JEAN exit. STELLA is tidying her hair in BARBIE-JEAN's mirror. Enter JAKE. He stares at her. She see him and stands still. Pause.

JAKE: What's go' into you Stella?

STELLA: Pardon?

JAKE: Wha' do ya wanna go to Torquay for? Come on. Perfect opportunity. Our Barbie-Jean away. Just us two.

He goes over to her. She moves away.

What's wrong?

Enter BARBIE-JEAN carrying toiletries.

BARBIE-JEAN: (*To JAKE.*) Wha' are ya doin' in me room ya smelly tramp?

JAKE: Nottin'.

BARBIE-JEAN: Ge' out soft lad. We 'ave to ge' ready.

JAKE: Wha'?

BARBIE-JEAN: Don't be comin' in me room when I'm away. I 'll find out. I can smell when you've been in 'ere.

JAKE: I'm not bothered.

> *JAKE takes his clothes out of the basket and exits. BARBIE-JEAN smiles at STELLA and puts on a CD. STELLA helps BARBIE-JEAN to pack a suitcase as they dance around to the music. BARBIE-JEAN picks up the Oscar Wilde book and thinks twice about packing it. Finally she puts it into the suitcase. Blackout.*

ACT 2

Scene 1

Wednesday, early afternoon. BARBIE-JEAN and STELLA are sunbathing on the beach in Torquay. Rather, STELLA is sunbathing and BARBIE-JEAN is sitting on a deckchair reading Oscar Wilde. STELLA is lying prostrate and wearing a bikini. BARBIE-JEAN is wearing short pants and a t-shirt, and also has a towel wrapped around her. The sound of seagulls and childrens' voices.

STELLA: Come for a swim Barbie-Jean.

BARBIE-JEAN: I already 'ave.

STELLA: No darling. That was a paddle. I mean a proper swim. (*She mimes.*)

BARBIE-JEAN: Too cold.

STELLA: You're just worried about your hair.

BARBIE-JEAN: I'm not.

STELLA: You're such a killjoy. Oh Barbie-Jean come on. It'll look fine once it's dried out.

BARBIE-JEAN: It won't. It'll look like a microwaved poodle.

STELLA: No change there.

BARBIE-JEAN: Tha' fuckin' sea water's not touchin' my 'ead.

STELLA: So you are worried about your hair.

BARBIE-JEAN: It's all set. I spent ages straightenin' it.

STELLA: It's full of sand anyway – probably.

BARBIE-JEAN: Don't remind me.

STELLA: You can't swim. You still need arm bands (*She laughs.*)

BARBIE-JEAN: Oh yeh. Like I wear a rubber ring in the shower.

STELLA: Come for a swim. You're such a bore. I'm not going on my own. Put some more lotion on my back then. Please. Go on.

BARBIE-JEAN: I'm tryna read.

BARBIE-JEAN rubs cream into STELLA's back.

STELLA: That's really cool. Arhh. Lovely. Further down. By my bum basically. Arhh yes.

BARBIE-JEAN: Don't 'ave an orgasm will ya? Would you like a foot massage as well?

STELLA: No thanks. Only lovers are allowed to touch my feet.

BARBIE-JEAN: Ya don't mind me slappin' white cream all over ya arse though.

STELLA: What's that book you're reading? I woudn't dream of bringing a book on holiday.

BARBIE-JEAN: Oscar Wilde.

STELLA: Who?

BARBIE-JEAN: Oscar Wilde.

STELLA: He was a singer wasn't he? I know he's dead.

BARBIE-JEAN: 'E was a writer ya divvie. Miss Parker…

STELLA: Oh – don't you mean, so obviously a dyke woman.

BARBIE-JEAN: So the' say.

STELLA: You're joking? The only person who doesn't know Miss Parker is a dyke, right, is Miss Parker.

BARBIE-JEAN: 'Ow can ya tell?

STELLA: Look at her. She makes Bob Hoskins look like Bambi, or something. Anyway, don't forget that little incident with you know who.

BARBIE-JEAN: Oh yer. I'm tellin' ya, if she touched me up in that stock cupboard, I'd batter 'er to death with the 'eaviest book available – probably the complete works of Shakespeare.

STELLA: She'd enjoy that. She'd turn it into a discussion about the meaning of darkness in *Twelfth Night*. If she touched me I'd kick her head in. And those 'relaxation exercises' she makes us do in drama.

BARBIE-JEAN: (*Mock teacher's voice as she continues to rub STELLA's back and buttocks.*) Girls, feel the tension draining away from your hips into the floor, just sinking away – the back of your skull getting heavier and heavier as it sinks deeper and deeper.

STELLA: What a lesbian. Mmmm. Rub some more cream in – lower down. It feels lovely when you do that.

BARBIE-JEAN: So, lesbian woman…

STELLA: Dyke woman.

BARBIE-JEAN: Dyke woman, right, wants me to 'read English' at university. I looked in this prospectus right, it said, funny enough, 'module in gay and lesbian writing'.

STELLA: There you are. See. She's trying to brainwash you.

BARBIE-JEAN: I thought, what's the point in 'avin' a module in gay and lesbian writing – all these writers are queer anyway.

STELLA: Rub harder babe. Harder.

BARBIE-JEAN: Do it yourself now. I wanna read.

She goes back to reading her book on the deck chair.

STELLA: I can't exactly rub cream on my own back. What do you think I am – deformed?

BARBIE-JEAN reads. STELLA sunbathes. Pause.

BARBIE-JEAN: Shit.

BARBIE-JEAN throws the book down and takes a mobile phone out of her pocket. She starts to play with it.

STELLA: What's up?

BARBIE-JEAN: Nottin'.

STELLA: (*Looking up. Sighs.*) You're not checking for messages again? This whole thing is like so gonna spoil your holiday. It's spoiling mine.

BARBIE-JEAN continues checking for messages.

If he's gonna call he'll call. Checking every five minutes won't make a difference. Maybe he wrote the number down wrong.

BARBIE-JEAN: 'E didn't.

STELLA: Just forget him.

BARBIE-JEAN: I can't. I feel guilty. The thought of 'im standin' there all night, on 'is own – waitin' for me.

STELLA: I bet you he's gone on holiday.

BARBIE-JEAN: 'E's got me number!

STELLA: So?

BARBIE-JEAN: I didn't turn up – 'e didn't call. 'E obviously thinks I'm not interested.

STELLA: Unlikely.

BARBIE-JEAN: What's that supposed to mean?

STELLA: Nothing. You never know. He might be in Torquay.

BARBIE-JEAN: Oh yer – who writes your scripts? Don't talk daft. Anyway, 'e's not a Speke-ite. 'E's from Crosby.

STELLA: So?

BARBIE-JEAN: So – 'e's not likely to go on 'olidee 'ere then is 'e? 'E'd go somewhere dead posh.

STELLA: Like where exactly?

BARBIE-JEAN: I dunno. Somewhere dead posh. Brussels.

STELLA: No one goes for a holiday in Brussels.

BARBIE-JEAN: Somewhere abroad.

STELLA: The Greek Islands probably.

BARBIE-JEAN: I 'ope 'e 'asn't gone there. Anyway, wha' are ya goin' on about? 'E's not in Greece – 'e's in fucking Crosby.

STELLA: With your mobile number. And a new girlfriend.

BARBIE-JEAN: Shut it bitch.

She flicks the towel at STELLA.

PAULINE: Let's party on down kids!

PAULINE appears. She is carrying her shoes, a handbag, a plastic cup containing cappuccino coffee, a small, pink ghetto blaster and an ice-cream. She is wearing huge earrings and her face is covered in cream.

BARBIE-JEAN: Don't Auntie Pauline. I feel ashamed!

PAULINE: Shut ya gob. I'll do wha' I like.

She starts singing along to the song playing from the ghetto blaster in a loud and unmusical voice.

STELLA: Are your burns any better Pauline?

PAULINE: Yes thank you love.

STELLA: Good.

PAULINE: (*She turns the music off.*) I should be able to stop usin' this cream by tonight. I just took me shoes off as I stepped onto the beach; this cheeky cunt goes to me, what's tha' cheesy smell, so I goes, your cock! Cheeky bastard.

She sits down.

'Ave yis been swimmin'?

STELLA: I have. Barbie hasn't.

PAULINE: Yiz wanna ge' a decent tan.

STELLA: I am.

PAULINE: (*Licking the ice cream.*) Mmmmm. Better than sex this? Still, I didn't come all this way for a fuckin' ice cream.

STELLA: Pauline – people can hear you.

PAULINE: Fuck 'em. An' who do ya think you are – the virgin Mary? Anyway, wha' 'appened to you shower o' bastards last night?

STELLA: What?

PAULINE: Leavin' me on me fuckin' own in the bar.

BARBIE-JEAN: I was there.

PAULINE: Not with me though. You spent all night prick sniffin'.

BARBIE-JEAN: I didn't.

PAULINE: You did. You was after tha' scruffy blond lad – Swampy!

BARBIE-JEAN: 'E's not scruffy.

59

PAULINE: Ya jokin' aren't ya. Tha' lad's never seen a bar o' soap in 'is life.

STELLA: I bet you'd like to give him a good washing down, wouldn't you Barbie-Jean.

BARBIE-JEAN: 'E's into funny music. That's all. 'E's no' a tramp.

PAULINE: Ya still didn't get 'is pants off.

BARBIE-JEAN: No. I got to meet 'im though.

PAULINE: Arh – goay. Useless.

BARBIE-JEAN: 'E'll be there tonight.

STELLA: Do you think you've got a chance Barbie-Jean?

PAULINE: No!

BARBIE-JEAN: Might 'ave.

PAULINE: (*To STELLA.*) Wha' 'appened to you?

STELLA: I was tired. That's all. Went back to the caravan for a lie down.

PAULINE: So, no-one's copped off.

STELLA: No.

PAULINE: Yis better get a move on then. We 'aven't got all week. Anyway, don't think yis are fuckin' off tonight – I need yis to make me look good in front o' tha' fella.

STELLA: What fella?

BARBIE-JEAN: 'E might just think you've go' loads o' daughters.

PAULINE: I look stupid sittin' there on me own.

STELLA: What fella?

PAULINE: The bloke behind the bar. 'E used to be in the Royal Marines – apparently. I'm in the mood for a bit o' seafood.

BARBIE-JEAN: Wha' – ya mean the one who looks like Mathew Corbett, from *The Sooty and Sweep Show*?

PAULINE: I think 'e's a cute. Anyway you can't talk.

BARBIE-JEAN: Wha' do ya mean?

PAULINE: Eyein' up tha' blond lad. We'll 'ave to start callin' you the child catcher.

Everyone laughs except BARBIE-JEAN.

BARBIE-JEAN: Piss off!

She storms off.

PAULINE: Barbie – we was only jokin' girl. Come back Barbie! Oh dear. There she goes.

STELLA: She's over-sensitive.

PAULINE: Nottin' wrong with bein' over-sensitive. In the right areas (*She laughs.*) I didn't mean to upset 'er.

STELLA: She'll come back.

PAULINE: I'm not like tha'. There's not one malicious bone in my body. I've gotta fuckin' malicious mouth though! (*She laughs.*)

BARBIE-JEAN returns.

BARBIE-JEAN: I left me book.

PAULINE grabs BARBIE-JEAN and hugs her.

PAULINE: What's up babe? We was only teasin' ya. We love ya really.

BARBIE-JEAN: I'm alright.

PAULINE: There's no need for tears. We're all gonna ge' the men we want. Any money. Let's make it official. Let's bet on it! Right, I'm goin' for Mathew Corbett, Barbie's on the case with Swampy… Stella?

STELLA: I'm keeping my options open.

PAULINE: Fair play. Now this is the deal. Let's 'ave a bit o' fun. I'm serious.

STELLA: Go on.

PAULINE: Whoever still 'asn't copped off by Fridee night, right, whoever's still a sad loser, okay, 'as to snog the ugliest bloke who's up for it – whichever one's available that night.

STELLA: Shouldn't be too difficult to arrange.

PAULINE: Are we on girls?

STELLA: Who chooses the bloke – the ugly one I mean?

PAULINE: I arrange it.

BARBIE-JEAN: An' 'ow ugly like?

PAULINE: Within reason.

BARBIE-JEAN: Yeh but – on a scale o' one to ten?

STELLA: What's ten?

BARBIE-JEAN: The elephant man.

STELLA: Seven?

BARBIE-JEAN: I dunno. John Prescott. Would you like me to draw a chart?

STELLA: I reckon you'll fix it Pauline.

PAULINE: I won't.

STELLA: You might choose someone really nice for yourself, if you end up…

PAULINE: If I end up the loser, God forbid, then you say who I 'ave to snog.

STELLA: We should make it a rule – he has to be under forty, at least.

PAULINE: Thirty!

STELLA: Fair enough. You're more experienced than us. You've got all the advantages of a mature woman.

PAULINE: Don't ya mean all the disadvantages of an old one?

BARBIE-JEAN: I'm not up for this.

STELLA: Why not?

PAULINE: Oh come off it Barbie!

BARBIE-JEAN: No chance! I'll end up losin'.

PAULINE: You've got a 'ead start – Swampy.

STELLA: Good point.

BARBIE-JEAN: So. I'm not getting off with some ugly old bloke.

PAULINE: Only if you 'aven't pulled by Fridee night.

STELLA: That's plenty of time.

PAULINE: Three nights.

BARBIE-JEAN: I don't care if it's three months. Or three years. I don't fancy John Prescott.

STELLA: He doesn't have to be that ugly.

BARBIE-JEAN: An' just 'ow far do we 'ave to go like?

PAULINE: As far as ya want.

BARBIE-JEAN: Wha' does tha' mean?

PAULINE: You only 'ave to snog 'im.

BARBIE-JEAN: What if 'e wants more?

PAULINE: Tell 'im it's not in ya contract.

STELLA: You're not gonna loose. Go on. It'll be fun. Go on.

PAULINE: You've got Swampy. 'E's in the bag. 'E's safe. 'E's yours. 'E's to take 'ome with ya – almost.

STELLA: Come on Barbie – it'll be a laugh.

BARBIE-JEAN: I don't know. I don't wanna one night stand anyway. It might be enough for youse two.

PAULINE: Look, ya won't 'ave to go back to 'is pad or anything, just in the club.

BARBIE-JEAN: It's like yis 'ave decided already – Barbie's gonna lose.

PAULINE: Look on the bright side, whatever the outcome, at least this way you've got more chance o' pullin' a fella this summer, if you so choose.

BARBIE-JEAN: Who says I'm desperate for one?

PAULINE: That's wha' we came 'ere for. Stop bein' a miserable bitch Barb. You're in an' that's it.

STELLA: It's sealed Barbie.

BARBIE-JEAN: You be quiet Moll Flanders.

PAULINE: Speakin' o' which, if all goes wrong, no one need be disappointed. I've been shoppin'.

BARBIE-JEAN: 'Ow do ya mean?

PAULINE: Right – Barbie, come 'ere.

BARBIE-JEAN: Wha'?

PAULINE: Come 'ere I said.

BARBIE-JEAN goes over to her.

Close ya eyes.

She does so.

'Old ya 'ands out.

She does so. PAULINE takes a vibrating dildo out of her handbag and puts it in BARBIE-JEAN's hands. It is battery operated and switched on. BARBIE-JEAN opens her eyes.

BARBIE-JEAN: Uurrghh! What's tha'?

She drops it onto the sand. PAULINE's laughter is hysterical.

PAULINE: It's a black mamba. Better than the white Russian!

BARBIE-JEAN: Oh my God!

STELLA: (*Serious.*) Auntie Pauline – everyone's looking – put it away quickly.

PAULINE: What's the matter with yis?

She picks it up.

They're jealous. That's all. They know someone's not gonna be disappointed tonight.

She starts waving it around at them, laughing uncontrollably.

BARBIE-JEAN: I can't believe 'er! She's on something.

STELLA: I wanna die. Please ground swallow me up now.

PAULINE: (*Still laughing.*) It's quite good for keepin' ya cappuccino nice an' frothy.

She dunks it in her plastic coffee cup. It splashes everywhere. Only PAULINE finds this funny – more so because the children are so horrified.

Who wants to borrow it first? Barbie? Stella?

STELLA: That's disgusting.

PAULINE: (*Laughing.*) You wait – yis'll be fightin' over it by tomorra night. Everyone'll be fightin' to stay in!

STELLA: I won't!

BARBIE-JEAN: I can't believe it.

PAULINE: Shall I bring it the club with me tonight?

BARBIE-JEAN: No way!

STELLA: No!

BARBIE-JEAN: I'm not goin' anywhere near 'er if she's go' tha' thing.

PAULINE: Come on you miserable bastards. We've got boys to catch! Boys, boys, boys. It's seventies disco night tonight. We'll 'ave a laugh! (*Looking up.*) It's gonna rain kids!

STELLA: Thank God.

BARBIE-JEAN: Let's go.

They pack up. PAULINE turns on her ghetto blaster. The music gets very loud and drowns out the noise of the beach, continuing into the next scene. Blackout.

Scene 2

Same day, 7.30pm. The interior of the caravan on 'Haven Caravans' holiday site. All that is needed is a long and thin sofa, curving round, with closed curtains above – to suggest a caravan. The rest is offstage. There is a small table in the centre, on top of which sits an assortment of makeup bags. Clothes are hanging up here and there and also strewn across the sofa. BARBIE-JEAN is applying makeup and looking into a small hand-held mirror. She is wearing a top with only one arm sleeve.

BARBIE-JEAN: You ready?

STELLA: (*Off.*) No. Does my skirt fit you?

BARBIE-JEAN: Don't be stupid. Anyway you might o' farted in it.

STELLA: (*Off.*) Pauline.

PAULINE: (*Off.*) Wha'?

STELLA: (*Off.*) Have I left my pencil liner in the toilet? I need it really badly.

PAULINE: (*Off.*) 'Ang on. Ya want me to wipe me arse don't ya?

BARBIE-JEAN: I'm gonna use the lip gloss.

STELLA: (*Off.*) You can't put lip gloss on with taupe. It looks stupid.

BARBIE-JEAN: I'm not wearin' the taupe.

STELLA: (*Off.*) What are you wearing?

BARBIE-JEAN: Pettle pink.

STELLA: (*Off.*) With those shoes?

PAULINE: (*Off.*) Where's the fuckin' bog roll? It's alright I've got it.

Enter STELLA. She is wearing a see-through top that does not cover her shoulders.

BARBIE-JEAN: Oh you're wearin' that.

STELLA: I thought you weren't using the pink any more.

BARBIE-JEAN: Pettle pink. What's wrong with it?

STELLA: Nothing. It's too flashy. For me, personally.

BARBIE-JEAN: Says a girl wearin' a see-through gypsy top.

STELLA: Are you wearing that slash-neck? Why don't you put your gypsy on?

PAULINE: (*Off.*) Yis better not be usin' all me fuckin' makeup.

Sound of toilet flushing.

BARBIE-JEAN: I don't like it. Shows too much.

STELLA: You can never show too much to a gorgeous guy. (*Rummaging through the make up.*) Why didn't you tell me you had foundation?

BARBIE-JEAN: It's Auntie Pauline's.

STELLA: Oh my God a blusher. (*Laughing.*) Does Pauline actually use this?

BARBIE-JEAN: I dunno.

BARBIE-JEAN tries it on her face. Enter PAULINE.

PAULINE: Careful with that. I use it to tickle me arse with.

BARBIE-JEAN: Thanks.

BARBIE-JEAN puts the blusher down and PAULINE hands the pencil liner to STELLA.

STELLA: (*Looking through different clothes.*) Do you think I should wear something else?

PAULINE: I 'ardly noticed you 'ad anything on. (*About the gypsy top.*) Wha' the fuck's tha' suppose to be?

BARBIE-JEAN: 'Elp me do me 'air somebody.

PAULINE: It's a bit small isn't it?

STELLA: It's meant to be.

PAULINE: I wouldn't be able to wrap me weddin' ring up in that.

BARBIE-JEAN: Where's the hairspray gone?

STELLA: It was here a minute ago.

PAULINE: We'll 'ave a laugh tonight – a proper girls' night out. Remember, if ya get a man, 'e's gotta buy ya stuff all week, an' ya don't want toiletries, ya want fuckin' diamonds.

STELLA is still checking out the various clothes, matching skirts with tops. PAULINE joins in and comments: 'That looks lovely – No, I don't like that.' BARBIE-JEAN finds the hairspray and struggles to apply it whilst holding the mirror at the same time: 'Can someone 'old this?' There is a knock on the door.

PAULINE: Who the fuck's tha' now? We're tryna ge' ready to go out 'ere.

She goes offstage to open the door.

Wha' the fuck are youse doin' 'ere?

STELLA: Who's that?

Enter PAULINE, KEVIN and JAKE, carrying cases. JAKE is wearing fishing gear and carrying a rod.

BARBIE-JEAN: Oh my God.

JAKE: Alright. Alright Stella.

STELLA is dumb-struck.

BARBIE-JEAN: That's me 'olidee ruined. Wha' 'ave yis come 'ere for? Yis can't stay 'ere.

KEVIN: Shut ya gob. (*About JAKE.*) 'E wouldn't stop pesterin' me. I 'ad to bring 'im down.

PAULINE: What's 'e dressed like a geriatric for?

JAKE: It's me fishin' gear.

PAULINE: An' wha' do ya think you're gonna catch down 'ere like, fish fingers?

BARBIE-JEAN: I 'ope 'e catches plague.

PAULINE: 'E's not gonna catch much else dressed like that.

BARBIE-JEAN: Does that mean you're goin' back right away?

KEVIN: Wha'?

69

BARBIE-JEAN: Does tha' mean you're goin' back? Now you've brought 'im down.

KEVIN: I've only jus' got 'ere. Make us a cup will ya? Anyway, I've got no work on for a few days. Thought I might stay.

BARBIE-JEAN: You're jokin'?

KEVIN: Wha'?

BARBIE-JEAN: The' can't stay in 'ere – with us.

JAKE: Why not?

BARBIE-JEAN: It's just us girls, isn't it Stella?

STELLA: (*Still overwhelmed.*) What?

STELLA exits to the toilet.

BARBIE-JEAN: There's no room.

JAKE: I don't mind sleepin' on the floor.

PAULINE: Yis can sleep on the sofa cushions.

BARBIE-JEAN: Auntie Pauline! Tell them no! Can't the' at least stay in a different caravan?

PAULINE: They'll all be booked up now.

BARBIE-JEAN: Oh! I don't believe it. (*To KEVIN and JAKE.*) Why do yis 'ave to spoil everything?

KEVIN: Listen madam, just 'cause you're on 'olidee…

PAULINE: We'll 'ave no fightin' in 'ere. Fuckin' shut up the lot o' yis.

JAKE: You 'eard Barbie.

PAULINE: You might 'ave told us you were comin'.

BARBIE-JEAN: Yeh. We'd 'ave gone out.

KEVIN: Thought it'd be a nice surprise.

BARBIE-JEAN: Nice surprise – oh yer – our Jake turns up smellin' like a dead fish and dressed like a total meff. You better not 'ave live bait in tha' basket.

JAKE: They're only maggots.

BARBIE-JEAN: Oh Jesus!

JAKE: The' can't get out.

BARBIE-JEAN: (*In tears.*) I'm not stayin' in this caravan with that stuff in 'ere! (*To JAKE.*) I 'ate you! You've ruined me 'olidee!

JAKE: Wha' 'ave I done?

BARBIE-JEAN: I 'ope you drop dead!

BARBIE-JEAN storms out of the caravan.

PAULINE: Barbie! Barbie!

KEVIN: Barbie – ge' back in 'ere before ya ge' a slapped arse!

PAULINE: Will you shut up? Wha' the fuck are ya lettin' 'im bring maggots in 'ere for? You know what she's like.

JAKE: Talk about an over-reaction.

KEVIN: I didn't know 'e 'ad them.

PAULINE: She only 'as to see one on the tele' an' she won't eat for fuckin' days.

JAKE: She's a spaz.

PAULINE: Get them fuckin' maggots out of 'ere now you. Where are the'?

JAKE: In a tub. In me basket. The' can't escape.

PAULINE: I don't fuckin' care. Just get them out.

KEVIN: 'Ere – give us the basket. I'll put it in the car.

PAULINE: I better go an' find Barbie.

They exit, still arguing. JAKE is on his own. Enter STELLA.

STELLA: Where is everyone? What's happened to Barbie?

JAKE: She's upset, about the maggots.

STELLA: What maggots?

JAKE: In me basket. Me fishin' basket.

Pause. STELLA folds up the clothes.

'Ave yis 'ad a good 'olidee like, so far?

STELLA: Yes.

JAKE: Wha' 'ave yis been doin'?

STELLA: Nothing.

Slight pause.

JAKE: I brought me fishin' gear down. I thought like, you know, Barbie 'ates fish. Do you wanna come fishin' with me tomorra?

STELLA: No thanks.

JAKE: We don't 'ave to catch fish or nottin' like. I just thought, it might be, you know, a good chance.

STELLA: I don't think so.

JAKE: Where do ya wanna go then?

STELLA: I'm not leaving Barbie on her own.

JAKE: She's got Auntie Pauline.

STELLA: Exactly.

JAKE: Oh come on. We could find somewhere quiet…

STELLA: No Jake.

JAKE: You want to don't ya?

Re-enter KEVIN and PAULINE with her arm round BARBIE-JEAN, who is tearful but no longer crying.

PAULINE: It's alright now love. (*To JAKE.*) Are you some sort o' fuckin' dick'ead bringin' that stuff in 'ere.

JAKE: I didn't know…

PAULINE: Ya fuckin' did. Don't lie. If I catch you with that stuff in 'ere again I'll fuckin' scrag you right out o' fuckin' Torquay, understand Jakey boy!?

JAKE: Yeh.

KEVIN: Leave the kid alone.

STELLA puts her arm round BARBIE-JEAN.

PAULINE: An' who are you all of a sudden – Jimmy Saville?

STELLA: You okay now Barb?

BARBIE-JEAN: Yeh.

KEVIN: 'E's got the picture.

PAULINE: Yis turn up out o' the fuckin' blue, bring a load maggots in 'ere, you upset our Barb…

KEVIN: Pauline, if ya don't stop goin' on we'll go back right now.

PAULINE: Piss off then!

KEVIN: Yeh, an' I'll take Barbie-Jean with me.

PAULINE: Ya fuckin' won't!

KEVIN: Do ya wanna bet on that?

PAULINE: Why don't yis just pissin' leave us alone.

KEVIN: Pack ya stuff then Barbie.

BARBIE-JEAN: No!

JAKE: Later Barb!

PAULINE: Will you stop bein' a fuckin' cunt – it's me who's 'avin' a go at you – not 'er. Leave Barbie out of it. Fuckin' big man you aren't ya, pickin' on a girl.

Slight pause. STELLA is still comforting BARBIE-JEAN. JAKE is emptying a stone out of his trainer.

Don't be fuckin' doin' that in 'ere!

JAKE: Sorry.

PAULINE: Who do ya think we are? The fuckin' flintsones? Fuckin' 'ell! Right, yis can sleep on the floor. Leave ya stuff in the kitchen. Take ya shoes off.

KEVIN: Alright Pol Pot. I thought this was an 'olidee camp. Not the killin' fields.

PAULINE: Is that why you brought a load o' maggots with ya? Don't worry Barb. They're in the car an' they're stayin' there.

BARBIE-JEAN: Just the thought o' them makes me wanna throw up.

PAULINE: Who – Kevin and Jake? I know 'ow ya feel.

STELLA: She meant the maggots.

PAULINE: So did I. Anyway, don't think you bastards are comin' out with us anywhere. This a girls' 'olidee.

STELLA: We were just getting ready to go out.

KEVIN: We can tag along can't we?

BARBIE-JEAN: No.

PAULINE: No ya can't. Girls' 'olidee means girls' night out. Girls as in no men.

KEVIN: I though that was the whole point of a girls' night out – eyin' up us blokes.

PAULINE: Yer, but not you ugly bastards.

KEVIN: Wha' are we gonna do?

PAULINE: Not our problem.

BARBIE-JEAN: Go fishin'. An' drown.

KEVIN: Alright madam.

JAKE: Yeh great. Fishin' at night. I've got me torch dad…

KEVIN: Shut up Jake. Ya can go fishin' tomorra. Don't think I'm goin' out on me own tonight. An' I'm certainly not stayin' in with 'im. (*Indicates JAKE.*)

PAULINE: Yis are not comin' with us, an that's that.

KEVIN: Extra drinks on me tonight.

PAULINE: I suppose it might solve the ugliest man in the club problem.

KEVIN: Ya wha'?

PAULINE: Nothing.

BARBIE-JEAN: Where ever youse two go, I'm goin' somewhere else.

KEVIN: That's right. Go off on ya own you miserable bitch.

BARBIE-JEAN: Me and Stella.

PAULINE: And me! Don't leave me with these two.

BARBIE-JEAN: You're comin' with us.

KEVIN: (*Taking the mickey.*) And take me. I wanna go!

JAKE: Me too!

KEVIN: Shut up.

PAULINE: Oh for fuck's sake. (*To BARBIE-JEAN and STELLA.*) We can't get rid o' these. (*To KEVIN.*) Look, if yis come with us, ya 'ave to do ya own thing. Ya can't be

75

'angin' round us all night, like flies. We've got other plans, 'aven't we girls?

JAKE: (*Looking at STELLA.*) Like wha'? Wha' plans?

PAULINE: Never you mind. We're doin' some fishin' of our own. You better find a sand pit to play in.

JAKE: I'm comin' with yis.

PAULINE: Oh fuckin' 'ell. We'll 'ave to go McDonald's in tha' case.

JAKE: I love McDonald's.

BARBIE-JEAN: Go on ya own.

PAULINE: Are we ready girls?

STELLA: Almost.

PAULINE: (*To KEVIN and JAKE.*) Ge' a move on then, if ya comin'. You 'ave to be fast to keep up with us.

KEVIN: I've left me shavin' kit in the car.

KEVIN exits.

PAULINE: I'll be in me room.

BARBIE-JEAN: Wha' are you doin'?

PAULINE: Just makin' a few final touches. Don't worry babe, I'll be back.

PAULINE exits. BARBIE-JEAN gets up to go.

STELLA: Where are you going?

BARBIE-JEAN: The toilet.

STELLA: You're not going to be sick are you?

BARBIE-JEAN: No.

She exits. Pause. STELLA deliberately turns her back on JAKE and aimlessly stacks up the remaining articles of clothes.

JAKE: Stella. Stella.

He goes over to her and holds her arm.

No-one's lookin'.

She turns round. They kiss. Blackout.

Scene 3

Same evening, 9pm in the on site 'club' at 'Haven Caravans'. KEVIN and BARBIE-JEAN are sat around the table. KEVIN has three pints of lager in front of him and is making a cigarette with tobacco and paper. BARBIE-JEAN is holding a trendy blue drink in a bottle. They are in a corner of the club. The lights from the dance floor intermittently sweep across them. Seventies disco music playing in the background.

BARBIE-JEAN: Don't know why you 'ave to smoke them things. Can't you smoke proper cigarettes? You look a right meff.

KEVIN: (*Enjoying his smoke.*) Shut it.

Pause.

Go an' 'ave a dance with Auntie Pauline.

BARBIE-JEAN: She makes a show o' ya.

KEVIN: She's 'avin' a good time – at least.

BARBIE-JEAN: I'm 'avin' a good time.

KEVIN: Oh yer. Sittin' there with an 'ead on ya like a robber's dog.

BARBIE-JEAN: What's tha' supposed to mean?

KEVIN: Cheer up. Don't ya like the music?

BARBIE-JEAN: I love it. It's dead sound.

KEVIN: Came out way before your time this stuff.

77

BARBIE-JEAN: I know.

KEVIN: I was courtin' ya mother.

BARBIE-JEAN: (*Depressed tone.*) I know.

Slight pause. BARBIE-JEAN looking across the bar.

Who's she onto now?

KEVIN: (*Looking round.*) Fuckin' 'ell. Stella's a bit of a tart isn't she? Anyway, 'ave you calmed down now, Miss Tilly Mint?

BARBIE-JEAN: Wha' do ya mean?

KEVIN: Screamin' ya fuckin' 'ead off all over the place.

BARBIE-JEAN: I'm not even sure if I can go back in the caravan.

KEVIN: Stop bein' melodramatic Barb.

BARBIE-JEAN: I'm not.

KEVIN: You are. Ya always 'ave been. Remember that time I took you to the pictures in town? You must o' been about eight.

BARBIE-JEAN: I remember goin' to the one in Runcorn. We went to see *Die Hard With A Vengeance*. It was dead stupid.

She takes a swig of her drink.

KEVIN: No this was in town. I left ya five minutes so I could go for a crap – when I came back, you were cryin' ya eyes out. You thought I'd gone 'ome without ya.

BARBIE-JEAN: Makes a change – me embarrassin' you.

KEVIN: You've got a phobia that's all. It runs in the family.

BARBIE-JEAN: Wha'?

KEVIN: This thing you've got abou' maggots.

BARBIE-JEAN: I just don't see why 'e 'as to bring 'em in the 'ouse.

KEVIN: Your gran' was scared o' cats. If she saw one in the street she'd run a mile.

BARBIE-JEAN: I remember.

KEVIN: It was a bit awkward like, if she was walkin' ya to school.

BARBIE-JEAN: I 'aven't exactly got a major problem dad, apart from our Jake.

KEVIN: 'E's alright. Leave 'im.

BARBIE-JEAN: I do, mostly. It's you tha' 'as a go at 'im for the most stupid things.

KEVIN: (*Laughing.*) Listen to you.

BARBIE-JEAN: I wish you'd lay off 'im. I know 'e's messy…

Enter PAULINE, sweating. She sits down.

PAULINE: That was great. Ge' up an' dance you two. (*Singing.*) Ge' up an' boogie. What's up with 'er?

KEVIN: Dunno. She's 'appy sittin' 'ere with 'er old man. Leave 'er.

PAULINE: Swampy's over there ya know.

BARBIE-JEAN: So is Mathew Corbett.

KEVIN: (*Jumping round.*) Where?

PAULINE: Not the real Mathew Corbett ya dick'ead.

KEVIN: Gonna say. You do sometimes ge' them in places like this.

PAULINE: Who's Stella chattin' up?

BARBIE-JEAN: Swampy's mate.

PAULINE: Which one – the dark 'aired lad?

BARBIE-JEAN: Yeh.

KEVIN: Ge' over an' talk to them.

PAULINE: Is Stella goin' after the dark lad?

BARBIE-JEAN: I think so.

PAULINE: She's talkin' to Swampy now.

BARBIE-JEAN: 'Is real name's Joe.

PAULINE: Eh – she's fixin' you up. You might be in with a chance girl.

BARBIE-JEAN: Oh God what's she sayin'?

PAULINE: Go over an' talk to 'em.

BARBIE-JEAN: I can't.

KEVIN: Ya only makin' friends.

BARBIE-JEAN: I don't know what to say to 'im do I?

KEVIN: 'Ello – my name's Barbie-Jean.

PAULINE: If you go round 'ere Kevin sayin' tha' you'll get kicked out. (*She laughs.*) There are separate clubs for men like you. (*To BARBIE-JEAN.*) Go on – go over before it's too late. Don't forget our little deal – remember? Now's ya chance.

KEVIN: What deal?

BARBIE-JEAN: I can't. I feel ashamed. 'E's seen me sittin' 'ere with you two.

PAULINE: Thanks a bunch. Don't be blamin' us 'cause ya can't talk to boys.

BARBIE-JEAN: I can.

PAULINE: Barbie-Jean you're worse than a bloke.

BARBIE-JEAN: 'Ow do ya mean?

PAULINE: I mean you're so fuckin' obvious when you fancy someone. You go all funny.

BARBIE-JEAN: I don't.

PAULINE: You do.

KEVIN: You leave my little girl alone.

Enter JAKE.

PAULINE: Be more relaxed. Don't take it so seriously.

KEVIN: (*To JAKE.*) Stay off the fuckin' lager you.

PAULINE: Don't be lettin' 'im drink tha' stuff in 'ere. We'll ge' kicked out.

JAKE: (*Sulkily.*) I don't care.

KEVIN: (*To JAKE.*) Not another one. What 'ave you got a gob on for? Wha' the fuck's wrong with my kids tonight?

PAULINE: I thought you met Swampy yesterday anyway.

BARBIE-JEAN: Briefly. We didn't say much. 'E's from Warrington.

PAULINE: Barbie-Jean – look!

BARBIE-JEAN: Wha'?

PAULINE: Stella's callin' you over.

BARBIE-JEAN: Oh no.

PAULINE: Go on.

BARBIE-JEAN: I can't.

PAULINE: She's wavin' at ya. Go on, ge' over there an' meet Prince Charming.

BARBIE-JEAN: Don't say that.

PAULINE: You like 'im don't ya?

BARBIE-JEAN: That's the problem.

KEVIN: Don't be encouragin' 'er too much. I don't wan' 'er like Stella.

PAULINE: Quick! The' might think you're bein' arrogant.

KEVIN: For God's sake Barb jus' go an' mix will ya. Jesus. Do ya wan' Jake to go over with ya?

BARBIE-JEAN: Alright I'm goin'.

She goes.

KEVIN: Thought that'd shift 'er fat arse.

PAULINE: Come on youse two. Come an' dance.

KEVIN: You've made enough cracks on the dance floor 'aven't ya?

PAULINE: I'll give you a fuckin' crack in a minute. You just gonna sit there, pourin' tha' shit down ya gob all night?

KEVIN: I'm keepin' an eye on me little girl.

PAULINE: I 'ope Stella 'asn't left our Barbie on 'er own.

KEVIN: She's okay.

PAULINE: Someone better go over there before she turns into fuckin' jelly. We'll 'ave to scrape 'er up off the fuckin' floor. (*She laughs.*) Come on ya fat bastard ge' up and dance. (*She grabs KEVIN's arm.*)

KEVIN: Goay girl.

PAULINE: Come on. Come 'ere.

KEVIN: Only one. Mind me drinks Jake.

PAULINE and KEVIN go to dance. STELLA comes over to the table to pick up her drink. She takes a swig.

STELLA: I'm going back over to Barbie.

JAKE: Watch it Stella.

STELLA: I beg your pardon?

JAKE: Talkin' dead posh won't change anythin'.

STELLA: I'm not listening to this.

JAKE: (*Grabbing STELLA's arm.*) Carryin' on like a…

STELLA: Like a what?

JAKE: Stella!

STELLA: Let go.

He does so.

Barbie might see. Or your dad.

JAKE: So wha'? They're gonna find out sooner or later.

STELLA: Find out what exactly?

JAKE: Abou' us.

STELLA: Jake – listen – I've told you, I don't want that.

JAKE: Doesn't excuse you getting off with other fellas!

STELLA: I haven't 'got off' with anybody.

JAKE: Ya tryin' though aren't ya?

STELLA: Jake – for God's sake, Barbie's gonna get suspicious. Look, listen, me and you, right, we had a laugh, that's all. Will you get it into your brain? – we are not a couple. We never were Jake. It was a one-off.

JAKE: Is three times a one-off?

STELLA: Jake, I did not come on holiday to be stalked by you.

JAKE: You've met someone else.

STELLA: I haven't met anybody!

JAKE: An' as for getting all worked up about Barbie-Jean…

STELLA: Barbie's my best mate.

JAKE: Is that why you've been tryna cop off with 'er fella?

STELLA: Who?

JAKE: The blond lad – Swampy.

STELLA: You don't know what you're talking about.

JAKE: Don't I? 'Is mate told me – you really fancy Swampy: Swampy really fancies you. 'E's not interested in our Barbie, an' who can blame 'im? I mean look at 'er.

STELLA: There's nothing wrong with her. She's a bit overweight that's all.

JAKE: Yeh. An' when it comes to chattin' up fellas, she's a retard. She 'asn't got a chance, an' you know it.

STELLA: I can't believe it – you think I'd like do that to Barbie?

JAKE: I don't care about Barbie.

STELLA: I do.

JAKE: She deserves everything she gets, or doesn't get. I 'ate 'er.

STELLA: No you don't.

JAKE: Wanna bet?

STELLA: Jake – I have no intention…

JAKE: You're the only reason I came to Torquay.

STELLA: Jake!

Enter BARBIE-JEAN.

That was a quick chat!

BARBIE-JEAN: Don't be silly. 'E's buyin' us a tequila – a tequila slammer. 'E wants to know if you want one.

STELLA: Okay.

BARBIE-JEAN: Isn't 'e gorgeous? This is the best night o' me life. 'Ave you seen them little beach sandals 'e's wearin'? 'Asn't 'e got lovely feet? An' 'e's a real blond you know.

STELLA: Yeh?

BARBIE-JEAN: Eh, ya won't believe it, 'e's dead interested to know where our caravan is, so I told 'im. 'E's only stayin' round the corner. Oh Stella I'm so 'appy. I'm in with a chance.

They hug each other.

'E likes me. Come on let's ge' back over there.

BARBIE-JEAN drags STELLA back over. JAKE watches. Enter PAULINE.

PAULINE: Where's the liver birds got to then eh?

JAKE: By the bar. With that lad.

PAULINE: Eh – it looks like our Barbie's gonna pull for a change. I 'ope so. She needs a boyfriend, badly. Poor girl's fuckin' desperate.

JAKE: Why does everyone always feel sorry for our Barbie?

PAULINE: 'Cause you always give 'er such a bad time.

JAKE: She gives me a bad time.

PAULINE: An' wha' about you Jakey boy? Anyone you like? Any fit girls? Suppose you're too young really aren't ya?

JAKE: Where's me dad?

PAULINE: 'E's up dancin', with this woman 'e knows from back 'ome.

JAKE: Who?

PAULINE: Over there. Never met 'er. 'Er name's Janet. She works in Lark Lane apparently, in some youth centre. She use to know ya dad's mum.

JAKE: What's she doin' down 'ere?

PAULINE: Same as us probably. Lookin' for a screw. 'E seems 'appy. So, we're the only two sad lonely 'earts. We'll 'ave to get together Jake.

She puts her arm round him and laughs.

JAKE: Ge' off!

PAULINE: Come for a dance then.

JAKE: No.

PAULINE: Come on. You might meet someone.

JAKE: Alright in a minute. I've gotta watch me dad's lager.

PAULINE: See you in a minute then.

She goes. JAKE looks around and then suddenly downs KEVIN's pints, one after the other. A loud burp. Blackout.

Scene 4

Later the same evening, 10.30pm. The ladies' toilets in the club at 'Haven Caravans'. The faint beats of dance music in the background. Enter BARBIE-JEAN. She goes over to a basin and tries to make herself throw up. No success. She covers her face with her hands, as if to hold back tears. Pause. Enter STELLA.

STELLA: Barbie, what's up?

BARBIE-JEAN: I can't even be sick.

STELLA: Don't be stupid.

STELLA comforts BARBIE-JEAN.

Don't make yourself sick.

BARBIE-JEAN: Easy for you to say.

STELLA: It's not my fault.

BARBIE-JEAN: That makes it worse.

STELLA: (*Laughing.*) How? This is so unfair.

BARBIE-JEAN: Who said anything about fair?

STELLA: Look, come back out and…

BARBIE-JEAN: (*Shouting.*) I feel stupid.

STELLA: Why?

BARBIE-JEAN: It's a bit fuckin' obvious isn't it? Well, obvious to everyone except me. You knew all along.

STELLA: Not necessarily.

BARBIE-JEAN: Not necessarily… Not necessarily: what the fuck is that supposed to mean?

STELLA: Barbie!

BARBIE-JEAN: You 'aven't exactly gone out o' your way to put 'im off – 'ave ya?

STELLA: Look, you can't say I've exactly encouraged him either.

BARBIE-JEAN: Couldn't you 'ave stayed away from this one, jus' for once?

STELLA: How could…

BARBIE-JEAN: You knew 'ow much I was into 'im.

STELLA: I don't believe this – you're makin' out it's all my fault, as if it's like, as if I've ruined every relationship you might have had.

BARBIE-JEAN: You knew from the first minute 'e was only interested in you – why didn't ya tell me Stella, why do you 'ave to drag me through the mud every time…

STELLA: What are you talking about? Barbie-Jean, when have I ever stood between you and, and some lad you wanted?

BARBIE-JEAN: 'Undreds o' times – probably. Ya crimes are just comin' to light.

STELLA: All I've ever tried to do is…

BARBIE-JEAN: (*Shouting.*) I feel a fool Stella!

Slight pause.

Can't you understand? I feel like the most stupid cow on God's earth!

STELLA: Barbie…

BARBIE-JEAN: Shut up! 'Ow can I go back in there an' talk to them lads? I'm a laughin' stock.

STELLA: You're not – if I thought…

BARBIE-JEAN: All the time I was bein' used! 'E only talked to me so 'e could get to you – you knew all along.

STELLA: You're being fucking paranoid Barbie. Quite frankly, how dare you suggest that I would behave like…

BARBIE-JEAN: Do you fancy 'im or not?

Slight pause.

STELLA: (*Unconvincingly.*) No. No.

BARBIE-JEAN: You do don't ya? All that shit about likin' butch men. It was a subterfuge.

STELLA: What?

BARBIE-JEAN: Read a book. I'm not bein' the clown any more. Fat chance. An' if you think I'm gonna be 'ere on

Fridee night, so you an' Pauline can 'ave a good laugh –
watchin' me snog some ugly bloke, forge' it. I'm goin'
'ome – tomorra.

STELLA: Barbie-Jean don't.

BARBIE-JEAN: I'm goin' back to the caravan, to read me
book.

STELLA: Don't!

STELLA intercepts BARBIE-JEAN.

BARBIE-JEAN: Piss off Stella.

STELLA: Please Barbie. I'm sorry. I'm sorry. I've been
stupid. I know it might seem… I know, I know I must
look like a right bitch. I'm sorry. I'm not used to this
situation. I should have told you this guy was a… Look,
I wasn't sure, to be honest. I mean, you think, you always
think I know more about what's going on than you do.
Alright I suspected, I suspected… For all I knew, he
might have been using me to get you. I wasn't sure.
(*Holding BARBIE-JEAN's arms.*) I never wanted you to get
hurt Barbie. Why won't you believe me?

STELLA cries. They hug each other.

I'm really sorry Barb.

BARBIE-JEAN: Don't cry babe. I'm sorry.

STELLA: What for?

BARBIE-JEAN: For bein' a bitch. It's not your fault. I
thought things'd be different down 'ere. It's just the same.
Ya fancy a lad, an' 'e's jus' not interested. An' the ones
tha' do like ya, they're dead ugly. (*Wiping STELLA's face.*)
Ya mascara's run all down ya cheeks. You can't go back
out like that.

STELLA: Look, Barbie, I promise, I'll have nothing to do
with him.

89

BARBIE-JEAN: Who?

STELLA: Swampy – and his mates.

BARBIE-JEAN: It's up to you…

STELLA: No. You're more important. I'm not throwing our friendship away for a one night stand. Why would I? Swampy's all yours, as far as I'm concerned.

BARBIE-JEAN: Look at the state o' ya. Wash ya face. I'll go an' ge' me make-up bag. I left it with Auntie Pauline. Do you up all nice again.

STELLA: Thanks.

They hug again and then hold hands.

BARBIE-JEAN: I'll ge' the make-up.

She exits. STELLA washes her face in a basin. Enter JAKE.

JAKE: Stella!

STELLA: Shit! Jake – get out! Don't come in the ladies.

JAKE: Why won't ya speak to me Stella?

STELLA: Get out Jake!

JAKE: I've been tryna catch ya eye. You won't even look at me.

STELLA: Jake, leave before Barbie gets back.

JAKE: I love you Stella!

STELLA: On no.

JAKE: I can't stop thinkin' about ya. I wanna marry ya!

STELLA: God this is all I need!

JAKE: I don't care wha' Barbie thinks – or me dad, or anyone! Let 'em think what the' like.

STELLA: Jake please go now.

JAKE: I know – ya only carryin' on like this 'cause we're on 'olidee.

STELLA: It's not…

JAKE: Tryna make me jealous, 'angin' round all them posh kids. You'll change when we ge' back to Liverpool. I know you really want me Stella. I'm not 'idin' anymore!

STELLA: No! Jake – just, look at you!

JAKE: Gorgeous aren't I?

STELLA: No, as a matter of fact, I can't stand you. Get out of here – quickly!

JAKE: Stella.

STELLA: I hate you! Can't you see? You're just a spotty little boy in a tracksuit. Get out of my face! Go!

JAKE: Kiss me Stella.

STELLA: I thought you were cute once, right, back in Speke, but not now – not here. Here you're just a… You make me puke!

He grabs her violently and pushes her against a cubicle door. They kiss and embrace passionately, STELLA no less enthusiastic than JAKE – his cap falls onto the floor. She tries to stop herself but can't. They are now inside the cubicle, having sex. Enter BARBIE-JEAN and PAULINE. STELLA slams the door but there is no lock and it keeps swinging open. Eventually they make it stay shut.

PAULINE: I've got this ladder in me tights, so 'e goes to me, is that a stairway to heaven, so I goes, no, it's a gateway to hell (*She laughs.*)

BARBIE-JEAN: (*Carrying the makeup bag.*) Stella?

PAULINE: Where's she got to? Eh, I tried one o' them tequilas with 'im. It was fuckin' funny; never 'ad one before. I kept pourin' the whole packet o' salt in me mouth.

BARBIE-JEAN: Stella?

PAULINE: She must o' gone.

STELLA: (*From the cubicle.*) I'm in here. Sorry.

PAULINE: Carry on with ya business babe. I'll join ya.

STELLA: Don't come in.

PAULINE: Don't be stupid. I'll use the one next door.

BARBIE-JEAN: You alright in there? I've got the makeup bag.

STELLA: There's no lock on the door. Make sure no-one comes in.

BARBIE-JEAN: Alright.

PAULINE goes into the cubicle next door.

PAULINE: Don't worry. I'm only droppin' a penny.

She closes the door. BARBIE-JEAN applies make up in the mirror. JAKE pulls his cap from under the cubicle door.

Fuckin' ell. There's great big 'ole in the wall. I can see right through into Stella's cubicle.

JAKE covers the hole with his hat.

Ya don't 'ave to cover it. I won't look.

STELLA: It's okay.

Silence. We can hear PAULINE urinating. BARBIE-JEAN continues to tidy up her make-up.

PAULINE: Jesus. I'm peein' like a fire-engine today.

Pause.

Oh fuck there's no toilet roll. Stella?

STELLA: Yes?

PAULINE: Wha' are ya doin' in there – 'avin' a baby? 'Ave you go' any bog roll?

STELLA: Just a minute.

PAULINE: Push some through this 'ole will ya?

She does so.

Tar.

PAULINE starts singing a Boney M number. Sound of the toilet flushing. Pause. PAULINE emerges from the cubicle.

Stella's been in there a while 'asn't she.

BARBIE-JEAN: (*Biting tissue to remove excess lipstick.*) Yeh.

PAULINE: You alright in there babe?

STELLA: Actually, I'm feeling really sick.

PAULINE: That's a shame.

BARBIE-JEAN: Do ya want me to come in?

STELLA: No. I'll be alright. Just leave me in here for a while. I'll be fine.

BARBIE-JEAN: I don't wanna leave you on ya own.

STELLA: No – go outside.

PAULINE: Are ya sure?

STELLA: If I need to be sick I don't want an audience.

PAULINE: Eh – do ya need the dildo? It's in me 'andbag.

Laughing, she takes it out and waves it around.

BARBIE-JEAN: Put it away quick – before someone comes in.

PAULINE: Let's wait for someone else to sit in tha' cubicle – then stick it through the 'ole (*She laughs.*)

BARBIE-JEAN: You're sick Auntie Pauline. Come on leave Stella alone. She's not feelin' well. We'll be in the bar Stella.

STELLA: Okay.

BARBIE-JEAN and PAULINE exit, the latter still laughing. Sighs of relief from STELLA and JAKE. Pause. The following conversation takes place from behind the cubicle door.

STELLA: Have you cum yet?

JAKE: Don't come in the ladies you said. No. 'Ave you?

STELLA: You must be joking.

JAKE: Do ya mind if we finish this later? I'm really uncomfortable.

Blackout.

Scene 5

Later on, around midnight. The caravan. JAKE and STELLA are having sex on the sofa. They are both very drunk. It is dark. STELLA's legs are wrapped around JAKE. They are virtually naked, except, absurdly, their underwear has been pulled down, rather than taken completely off. Clothes are scattered about the floor. Enter BARBIE-JEAN carrying a bag of chips. The light goes on.

JAKE: Don't you ever knock Barbie-Jean?

BARBIE-JEAN: Jesus.

JAKE: (*Pulling up his underwear.*) You 'ave to be in on everythin', don't ya?

BARBIE-JEAN: Stella.

STELLA: Oh no.

JAKE: Leave 'er.

BARBIE-JEAN: (*Laughing.*) I thought you 'ad standards.

JAKE: Ge' out Barbie. This is private.

STELLA, in a very drunken and clumsy fashion, attempts to get dressed – unsuccessfully.

BARBIE-JEAN: It's a communal caravan dick'ead. If ya gonna make fools o' yourselves couldn't yis use the beach? An' I can't find Swampy anywhere.

JAKE: Ge' out Barbie!

BARBIE-JEAN: Oh Stella – wha' are ya doin' – avin' it off with the maggot king? I looked up to you.

JAKE: Shut it Barb!

BARBIE-JEAN: Where's all the butch men?

JAKE: Not with you.

BARBIE-JEAN: I only came back for me Oscar Wilde book. I suppose you've 'ad sex with 'im as well.

STELLA: I was meaning to tell you Barbie.

BARBIE-JEAN: I can see why ya didn't want to.

JAKE: Don't ya mean, I wanted to tell 'er. (*Pointing to STELLA.*) She wouldn't let me. I knew this was gonna 'appen.

STELLA: Be quiet Jake. You've got, look, you wanted everyone to find out – now they have.

BARBIE-JEAN: I won't say anything.

STELLA: We're still friends aren't we Barb?

BARBIE-JEAN: You need friends at a time like this. (*She laughs very loudly.*) Sorry.

STELLA: (*Crawling around on the floor looking for clothes.*) It's not serious or anything.

JAKE: Shut up you. It is serious. (*To BARBIE-JEAN.*) It is serious!

BARBIE-JEAN: Seriously funny. I can't believe it.

STELLA: What?

BARBIE-JEAN: I feel responsible, some 'ow, like, I could 'ave done more to prevent it (*She laughs again.*)

JAKE: At least she's still not a fuckin' virgin.

BARBIE-JEAN throws the bag of chips at JAKE.

STELLA: Shut up Jake.

Slight pause.

BARBIE-JEAN: Say tha' again.

JAKE: Wha'?

BARBIE-JEAN: Go on, I dare ya. Say tha' again.

JAKE: You 'eard. Yeh. At least she can ge' a boyfriend.

STELLA: Don't go there Jake!

BARBIE-JEAN: I'm choosey – that's all!

JAKE: Choosey my arse. I'll tell why ya can't ge' laid, 'cause you're too fat an' ugly, an' you're a selfish bitch. No-one likes ya. Face the truth Barbie-Jean.

STELLA: You bastard.

JAKE: You don't even know, ya can't even see 'ow stupid you look – chasin' round that blond lad all night, like some big fat cow, as if you 'ad chance! Do you 'onestly think, did you think for a minute tha' 'e would ge' off with you? Look at the state o' ya!

STELLA: Don't Jake.

JAKE: A fuckin' hungry hippo – tryna dress up as a doll. You look fuckin' ridiculous – ya fuckin' fat arse stickin' out all over the fuckin' place. (*He laughs.*) Them lads 'ave been laughin' at ya – behind ya back. Barbie, if you were the only bird in a bloke's prison – ya still couldn't ge' laid.

STELLA: That's it. I'm finished with you.

She goes over to BARBIE-JEAN and holds her hand.

JAKE: You shut up an' all you big fuckin' tart. Actin' like butter wouldn't melt in ya mouth.

BARBIE-JEAN: You leave 'er out o' this.

JAKE: Ah goay. Stella, ya might talk posh, but, we all know, your shit's been stabbed by every bloke on this caravan site – except, you 'aven't got to the rest o' Torquay yet!

STELLA: You said you wanted to marry me!

STELLA cries on BARBIE-JEAN's shoulder.

JAKE: Marry ya! Stella, if I stuck this caravan up ya arse, you wouldn't notice. You're the 'olidee camp bike – everyone's 'ad a ride.

BARBIE-JEAN: You better shut your fuckin' mouth!

JAKE: I don't know wha' you're defendin' 'er for. She's cheated both of us.

BARBIE-JEAN: 'Ow do ya mean?

JAKE: Ask Swampy?

BARBIE-JEAN: Wha' about Swampy?

JAKE: She 'ad it off with 'im last night – in 'is caravan.

BARBIE-JEAN lets go of STELLA's hand.

BARBIE-JEAN: Ya wha'?

JAKE: Ask 'im, if ya don't believe me. Not tha' 'e'd ever 'ave slept with you anyway Barbie. 'E told me, 'e said like, no offence, but your sister, she is a dog. I 'ad to agree. One o' ya fake eyelashes 'as fallen off – you look stupid, or should I say, more stupid.

BARBIE-JEAN: Right, now you've 'ad your say, I'm 'avin' mine – ge' out o' this fuckin' caravan!

JAKE: Ge' off Barbie!

She pushes JAKE out of the caravan and locks the door; he is kicking and shouting and wearing only his underpants.

JAKE: (*Banging on the window from outside.*) Le' me in!

BARBIE-JEAN: (*To STELLA.*) Listen bitch – you're gonna ge' fuckin' murdered in 'ere tonight!

STELLA: No Barbie!

STELLA tries to escape out of the door but she is too drunk and BARBIE-JEAN pushes her onto the floor. JAKE is still banging on the windows from outside.

BARBIE-JEAN: This is your fuckin' big sacrifice is it?

STELLA: (*Slightly aggressive.*) I didn't want things to turn out like this Barbie!

BARBIE-JEAN: You couldn't keep ya greasy fingers off Swampy could ya? There's no stoppin' you.

STELLA: It's not my fault!

BARBIE-JEAN: No-one 'as sex by accident Stella. We made a deal. Don't you 'ave any fuckin' limits? Who's it gonna be next, me dad?

STELLA: (*Standing up.*) It had already happened Barbie...

BARBIE-JEAN: Jake's right about one thing – you're the sexual equivalent of a combine harvester. You'd shag your own father if you knew who 'e was!

STELLA: How dare you!

BARBIE-JEAN: Isn't it about time you stopped tryna ge' back at your mum by shaggin' everything tha' moves?

STELLA: At least I speak to my mum!

BARBIE-JEAN: Stella, you know it, you've been carryin' on like this ever since you found out you were a bastard. No amount of voice elocution lessons can change that! All you can do is drag everyone down with ya!

STELLA: That's your department Barbie! Why is it always everyone else's fault that you can't find a boyfriend? Do you ever think, does ever occur to you, has it ever once entered your head, the reason you can't get laid – is you! You Barbie! You're such a control freak…

BARBIE-JEAN: An' you're not – you're the biggest fuckin' manipulator this planet's ever fuckin' known!

STELLA: Barbie – your personality is your most effective form of contraception!

BARBIE-JEAN: You need help Stella!

STELLA: Yeh?!

BARBIE-JEAN: Yeh, you need help – 'cause I'm gonna scrag your 'ead all over this fuckin' caravan. Bitch!

Within seconds BARBIE-JEAN is on top of STELLA: STELLA is screaming and JAKE is shouting from outside. He breaks through the door and tries to pull BARBIE-JEAN off STELLA. All three of them are struggling and screaming when suddenly, standing up and in the middle, STELLA pisses herself. The other two watch in panic. STELLA stands still as she cries and pisses down her leg and over the carpet.

JAKE: What's she doin'?

BARBIE-JEAN: Cleanin' the carpet. What does it look like? It 'appens every time she gets drunk.

JAKE: Ya never told me.

BARBIE-JEAN: Yeh. She just cries and pisses 'erself.

The caravan door is wide open.

PAULINE: (*From outside.*) Eh you ya shower o' fuckin' bastards. Come on – fuckin' Stella ya fuckin' bitch!

KEVIN runs through the door. STELLA is still crying.

JAKE: What's goin' on?

KEVIN: It's Auntie Pauline. I can't control 'er. She's pissed. Mathew Corbett turned 'er down. Said 'e preferred Stella; she battered 'is face with the dildo.

JAKE: (*Looking outside.*) She's tryna ge' in to the wrong caravan.

PAULINE: (*Outside.*) Eh youse fuckin' gypsy bastards. Where's Mathew Corbett then eh?!

JAKE: (*At the door.*) She's got 'old o' some old geezer in pyjamas. She's attackin' 'im with the dildo!

KEVIN: I better go an 'elp 'im.

STELLA collapses.

What's up with 'er?

PAULINE: (*Outside.*) Stella! Stella darling!

BARBIE-JEAN: Never mind! Jus' make sure Auntie Pauline doesn't find Stella.

KEVIN goes out.

PAULINE: Stella – where are ya? Ya bitch! I'll fuckin' eat ya when I ge' 'old o' ya. I'll fuckin' eat ya! Eat! Do you 'ear me?

JAKE: She's comin' over now!

BARBIE-JEAN: Quick. 'Elp us lift Stella onto the toilet.

They both try to lift STELLA.

She'll be safe as long as Auntie Pauline doesn't see 'er.

Suddenly PAULINE is banging on the window, KEVIN trying to pull her away.

PAULINE: I can see yis ya shower o' bastards! Don't be tryna fuckin' 'ide from me!

KEVIN: Fuckin' calm down will ya!

BARBIE-JEAN drops STELLA as she trips over a shoe.

JAKE: Quick! She's comin' in.

Suddenly the dildo is hurled through the open door, stopping JAKE and BARBIE-JEAN in their tracks.

PAULINE: (*Still outside.*) Eh you fuckin' Mathew Corbetts – ge' out 'ere now youse.

KEVIN: Pauline – calm down!

JAKE: Quick Barbie-Jean.

BARBIE-JEAN: I'm tryin'!

Just as BARBIE-JEAN and JAKE are passing the door PAULINE collapses into the caravan, falling on top of an unknowing STELLA. KEVIN enters. They all stand still. Silence. PAULINE starts snoring.

JAKE: (*Sniffing his hands.*) Me fingers stink o' piss.

BARBIE-JEAN goes to leave through the door, book in hand.

KEVIN: Where are you goin'?

BARBIE-JEAN: To the beach – to look at the lights; an' finish readin' me play.

BARBIE-JEAN exits. JAKE nods his head and goes off to the bathroom. KEVIN stands staring at STELLA and PAULINE lying on the floor, fast asleep and snoring. Music from a radio in the bathroom: 'Zoom' by Fat Larry's Band. KEVIN tidies up the mess. Blackout.

Scene 6

Next morning, Thursday. The caravan. BARBIE-JEAN sits on the sofa reading her book. She is dressed and ready to go out.

PAULINE: (*Offstage.*) Do want jam on this toast Barbie?

BARBIE-JEAN: Yes please.

PAULINE: It's burnt. 'Ang on. Should be alright.

Pause. She brings the toast in on a plate to BARBIE-JEAN.

BARBIE-JEAN: Tar.

She reads as she eats the toast.

PAULINE: I can't believe it. I just can't ge' over it.

BARBIE-JEAN: Yeh.

As BARBIE-JEAN reads PAULINE tidies up around the caravan.

PAULINE: Don't be all day will ya?

BARBIE-JEAN: I'm goin' out soon.

PAULINE: It can't be 'ealthy.

BARBIE-JEAN: Wha'?

PAULINE: You with ya 'ead stuck in a book all day. You'll end up getting big ideas – thinkin' you're too good to do proper work. Come on shift ya arse. I wish these bastards would ge' up. I wanna clean this caravan. Lets' put some music on. Wake the whole camp up.

Enter KEVIN from the door.

Where the fuck 'ave you been? You're worse than the kids. We wanna get ready. Where were ya?

KEVIN: Nowhere.

PAULINE: Oh thanks. You turn up outta the fuckin' blue last night, an' then piss off without tell anyone where ya goin'. Do us favour, try communicatin' with people in future.

KEVIN: Alright; what's up with you?

PAULINE: I've got things to do 'aven't I? I can't sit around all day waitin' for you to turn up.

KEVIN: It's only early.

PAULINE: So where were ya? You didn't sleep in the car – 'cause ya weren't there when I looked this mornin'. Unless you went to the shop.

KEVIN: Okay.

PAULINE: Where were ya then?

BARBIE-JEAN: We thought you'd been kidnapped.

PAULINE: We weren't tha' optimistic.

KEVIN: Wha' are yis complainin' for. More room in the caravan wasn't there?

PAULINE: I'm sure that's no' the fuckin' reason ya stopped out all night. Who where you with?

KEVIN: Janet.

BARBIE-JEAN: Where?

KEVIN: In 'er caravan – it's on the' other side o' the camp.

BARBIE-JEAN: Wha' were ya doin' there?

KEVIN: Mind ya own business.

PAULINE: Goay. Wait till Angie find out about this!

KEVIN: We didn't do anything. Just talked – that's all. 'Er mate 'ad to go back to Kirby yesterdee. Doesn't like sleepin' on 'er own.

PAULINE: I bet she doesn't.

KEVIN: I stayed in the spare room. (*To BARBIE-JEAN.*) Wha' are you lookin' at?

BARBIE-JEAN: Nottin'.

PAULINE: She's probably jealous. We all thought we'd be sorted by now, an' who ends up findin' the perfect love match – father feck over there.

KEVIN: Perfect love match! Goay.

PAULINE: That reminds me.

KEVIN: Wha' now?

PAULINE: We've got something to tell ya.

KEVIN: What is it?

PAULINE: (*Shouting.*) Jake! Stella! Come on ge' up. I've made yis breakfast!

JAKE: (*Offstage.*) 'Ang on!

PAULINE: Come on 'urry up. It's ready (*laughing.*).

JAKE emerges wearing only shorts.

Where's Stella?

JAKE: She's comin' now. Where's breakfast?

PAULINE: I 'aven't made it yet. (*Laughing.*) I will in a minute though. I just want ya dad to see. Stella!

JAKE: See wha' like?

STELLA emerges in a nightdress. She stands next to JAKE, yawning.

Oh yer.

STELLA leans on JAKE. He puts his arm around her.

So what's for breakfast?

They sit down.

PAULINE: (*To KEVIN.*) An' you can't 'ave a go at 'im.

KEVIN: I wasn't goin' to.

PAULINE: 'Cause you're just as bad – getting off with an older woman! (*Laughing.*).

KEVIN: Will you shut up? I 'aven't said anything 'ave I?

PAULINE: At least they're closer in age than you an' Janet!

KEVIN: Give ya arse a rest! I don't care. 'E can do wha' 'e likes.

PAULINE: Who wants toast?

JAKE: Me please.

PAULINE exits to the kitchen. JAKE clutches STELLA's hand.

Do you wan' toast?

STELLA: Yes please.

JAKE: Stella wants toast.

PAULINE: (*Offstage.*) Okay.

STELLA picks up a magazine from the coffee table and reads. The characters should either be reading or sitting saying nothing. PAULINE comes back on stage.

Toast'll be ready in a minute. Listen, I've got something to tell yis.

Everyone pays attention.

JAKE: What's up?

PAULINE: Gotta call early this mornin' didn't I – from the police. John's in 'ospital again. 'E called round to see Kerry an' the baby; she told 'im to piss off, so 'e went on a massive fuckin' drinkin' binge. I don't care like. I don't care wha' 'appens to 'im. It's just, 'e might need me there, ya know.

KEVIN: 'E'll be alright.

PAULINE: No, listen, I don't want anyone getting a cob on – there's no need for this to effect youse, I mean yis can stay 'ere until Saturday, if ya like, it's just, I can't, if 'e's in 'ospital, I've gotta be there. I'm goin' back today.

JAKE: Oh don't go today.

BARBIE-JEAN: Wha' about Fridee night?

PAULINE: Wha'?

BARBIE-JEAN: Fridee night – remember – our big night!

PAULINE: Get real Barbie.

KEVIN: Let 'im ge' on with it girl. We've been tellin' 'im for years....

PAULINE: An' wha' would you know? Anyway, I've already packed me things. I'm getting the twelve o' clock train, an' that's final.

She goes back into the kitchen.

BARBIE-JEAN: It's a shame.

KEVIN's mobile rings. He answers it.

KEVIN: 'Ello. Alright mate. Yeh. Yeh. Go on. No I don't mind. Yeh. I see. Thanks. I'll be back tomorra. Alright thanks Matty. See ya.

He puts the mobile away.

That was Matty. I gave 'im the keys so 'e could check for messages, while we're away like. Apparently, a letter's arrived from your school Jake – addressed to me.

JAKE: Oh yer.

KEVIN: Oh yer.

Slight pause.

Ya know wha' it's about don't ya?

JAKE: Yeh. I think so. Is it about me getting suspended?

KEVIN nods.

Sorry.

KEVIN: Sorry? Is tha' all you've got to say for yourself –
sorry?

PAULINE emerges with burnt toast.

Do you think you can 'ide things like tha' from me?

JAKE: Obviously not.

KEVIN: Obviously. You must think I'm stupid.

PAULINE: Sorry everyone – it's a bit burnt. Tha' toaster's a
fuckin' furnace.

She puts the plate of toast down on the table.

It's like a charnal 'ouse in 'ere. I'll open some windows.

She exits. Slight pause.

JAKE: Aren't ya gonna go mad at me?

KEVIN: I've a good mind to take ya back right now. Only
why should I ruin my 'olidee because o' you?

PAULINE: (*Off.*) Plus 'e's got Janet.

KEVIN: Shut it you.

Slight pause.

Nottin' I can do. You've been suspended already. It's your
future lad. I've got me own problems.

*BARBIE-JEAN looks sheepishly over her book. STELLA reads
the magazine. JAKE and KEVIN sit eating burnt toast.*

PAULINE: (*Off.*) Don't be sittin' there all day. Yis better
keep this place clean an' all, after I've gone.

They finish eating the toast. KEVIN carries the plate in to PAULINE.

KEVIN: (*Off.*) No time for a cuppa?

PAULINE: (*Off.*) Make it ya self. Be quick. I'll 'ave one. Two sugars.

KEVIN: (*Off.*) Anyone want tea?

JAKE: Yes please. An' Stella.

BARBIE-JEAN: Not for me. I've already 'ad one. Don't wanna be pissin' meself all mornin'.

Suddenly remembering last night and looking at STELLA.

Sorry.

Pause.

STELLA: Barbie?

BARBIE-JEAN: Yeh?

STELLA: Me and Jake, well, we were thinking of like, we might go to the Riviera Centre today. Do you want to come with us?

BARBIE-JEAN: Wha' do ya wanna be stuck in there for – there's a lovely beach outside? No tar.

STELLA: Come on it'll be a laugh. There's a big slide in the swimming pool.

JAKE: She'll ge' stuck in it.

BARBIE-JEAN: Ho ho Jake. No. I'm alright. There's some books I wanna buy in town.

JAKE: Wha' are ya gonna do all day – jus' read books? You're goin' off ya 'ead you. You're suppose to be 'avin' fun. You're on 'olidee.

BARBIE-JEAN: I am 'avin' fun.

JAKE: Doesn't look much like it to me.

BARBIE-JEAN: There's a little café down by the 'arbour. Ya can sit outside an' watch the boats. It's lovely. I'll be down there if yis get bored playin' on the slide.

JAKE: If we ge' bored? More like you will.

BARBIE-JEAN: Don't think so.

STELLA: Hey Barbie, there's some nice lads down the Riveria Centre. You never know....

BARBIE-JEAN: Thanks for your concern Stella, but I'm really no' interested. I've 'ad enough o' tha' game. There are better things to do.

JAKE: What's 'appened to 'er?

STELLA: She must have met Mr Right on the beach last night.

BARBIE-JEAN: You could say that. Only he's been dead for over a 'undred years.

STELLA: What?

JAKE: I wouldn't put it past 'er to cop off with a corpse.

BARBIE-JEAN: Unlikely. 'E's buried in Paris.

JAKE: Paris?

BARBIE-JEAN: Let's just say the sea air cleared me 'ead a bit.

JAKE: More like gone to ya 'ead.

BARBIE-JEAN: I'm not bein' condescendin' or nottin', but yis wouldn't understand. I've got me priorities in order. I wanna be a writer.

Laughter from STELLA and JAKE.

JAKE: Stop it Barb'.

STELLA: You do make us laugh Barbie-Jean.

JAKE: Eh Auntie Pauline, our Barbie's gonna write books. What, like, cookery books?

Laughter.

Just desserts eh?

Laughter.

BARBIE-JEAN: You said it boy.

JAKE: Wha'?

BARBIE-JEAN: Nottin'.

JAKE: (*Wiping the tears from his eyes.*) You're a killer Barb'.

BARBIE-JEAN: You two go and play now. I've got stuff to do.

STELLA and JAKE look at each other.

STELLA: I better get ready Jake.

She stands up.

Might see you later Barbie.

BARBIE-JEAN: Yeh. Okay. 'Ave a good time.

STELLA and JAKE go. BARBIE-JEAN sits reading. Blackout.

ACT 3

Speke, Liverpool. Three months later. Late October. Sunday morning. The weather is sunny and mild; the last traces of summer. A back garden with three chairs. KEVIN, wearing dungarees and plastic gloves, is standing in the middle of the garden holding a mug of tea in one hand and talking into his mobile phone on the other.

KEVIN: (*Into mobile.*) Janet – no, look, listen; I 'aven't told 'er yet. It won't be easy ya know. 'Er mum's not been gone long. The idea of you movin' in now – I know what Barbie-Jean's like. She'll kick off. Alright. Alright. I'll tell 'er today. Promise. Speak to ya later. Love ya.

KEVIN puts his phone away, looking around and taking in the sun. BARBIE-JEAN breezes in and sits on a chair. She is carrying the Oscar Wilde book, a book of Wordsworth's poetry, a notebook and a batch of university prospectuses. Her accent is now mild and she is making an effort to talk 'properly'.

Where's Jake?

BARBIE-JEAN: Gone out.

KEVIN: Where?

BARBIE-JEAN: I don't know. Tony's probably. Not likely to go and see Stella is he?

KEVIN: Not likely luv.

Pause.

Are you sure ya don't know nottin'?

BARBIE-JEAN: No; I've told you. I know about as much as Stella. Let's just say, look in the Torquay telephone directory – take your pick.

KEVIN: It's not our Jake's.

BARBIE-JEAN: If you're sure.

KEVIN: Look, 'e's told me it's not 'is, an' that's all I've got to go on.

BARBIE-JEAN: Stella's dad doesn't agree.

KEVIN: I know. Well, ya know Jake's story, ya know, they never went tha' far, an' all that. Unless you know something I don't know.

BARBIE-JEAN: How could I? I wasn't there watching with score cards. Actually it was a bag of chips.

KEVIN: Wha'?

BARBIE-JEAN: Nothing.

KEVIN: If it does turn out to be Jake's, God I'd kill 'im. I mean if 'e abandoned 'er.

BARBIE-JEAN: Yep.

KEVIN: There's been enough o' tha' round 'ere lately.

BARBIE-JEAN looks at him sharply.

What's tha' shit ya readin'?

BARBIE-JEAN: University Prospecti.

KEVIN: You 'ave to pass ya A-Levels first.

BARBIE-JEAN: Look!

BARBIE-JEAN shows KEVIN all the work she has done in the notebook.

KEVIN: Oh well done. Is it finally sinkin' in?

BARBIE-JEAN: I'm all prepared for my interview with the careers officer.

KEVIN: Am I finally getting through to ya girl? Never mind university prospecti – pass ya exams first.

BARBIE-JEAN: You don't understand do you?

KEVIN: No I'm thick.

BARBIE-JEAN: You have to start applying to places this year.

KEVIN: An' wha' 'appens if ya fail ya exams?

BARBIE-JEAN: You go to an execrable university. (*Pleased with herself for having used a big word.*)

KEVIN picks up some of the prospectuses.

KEVIN: Wha'?

BARBIE-JEAN: Not me. I know what I want.

KEVIN: (*Reading.*) Oxford! Ya jokin' aren't ya girl? You're no' clever enough to go there.

BARBIE-JEAN: I am.

KEVIN: Ya 'ave to be dead brainy. Or dead rich – you're neither.

BARBIE-JEAN: I'm not applying to Oxford. There's plenty of better places.

KEVIN: Like where?

BARBIE-JEAN: I'm looking.

KEVIN: You'll end up in Liverpool Poly.

BARBIE-JEAN: There's no such place.

KEVIN: Livin' at 'ome with daddy.

BARBIE-JEAN: I'm not staying in Liverpool. That's for certain. I thought I might, but, after the holiday in Torquay, I realised, well, I want to go somewhere else. I want a change. It was lovely down there – the lights at night time, right along the beach; and the houses, painted all nice – rose pinks, all lemons and limes; really exquisite. I'll go down south.

KEVIN: An' wha' are ya gonna study?

BARBIE-JEAN: English.

KEVIN: Ya 'ave to be able to read an' write first.

BARBIE-JEAN: Funny. I've told you, I'm going to read and write.

She reads a prospectus.

KEVIN: Auntie Pauline should be 'ere soon.

BARBIE-JEAN: Oh no.

KEVIN: Can I ge' you a cup?

BARBIE-JEAN: No tar. No thank you.

She continues reading.

KEVIN: Interestin'?

Pause.

Barb, put the book down.

BARBIE-JEAN: Prospectus.

KEVIN: Don't start. Whatever.

BARBIE-JEAN: (*Putting the prospectus down.*) What is it?

KEVIN: Just – listen a minute.

BARBIE-JEAN: Well?

KEVIN: You know – you know Janet, right?

BARBIE-JEAN: What about her?

KEVIN: Well – you know, right, I've been seein' 'er since the 'olidee in Torquay?

BARBIE-JEAN: I know that.

KEVIN: No listen. We ge' on really well right, an', she's go' a good job an' everythin'. It's just – she's livin' in this flat on 'er own, actually it's 'er ex-boyfriend's place. No good to 'er. We were thinkin', right, you know she works in

Lark Lane, it'd be quite 'andy, for the bus, we were thinking, well, she could move in with us. Wha' do ya think? She's dead clean an' everythin' – she'd be 'andy round the 'ouse like. She can cook as well.

BARBIE-JEAN: I can cook!

KEVIN: I know, but, well, wha' do ya think babe?

BARBIE-JEAN: What about mum?

KEVIN: Wha' about 'er?

BARBIE-JEAN: What's she going to say?

KEVIN: I don't know. She's no' 'ere is she? Do you see 'er anywhere?

BARBIE-JEAN: Yes but, you can't just…

KEVIN: Angie's no' comin' back Barbie-Jean. Your mum's left ya. That's all there is to it. Face facts. Face facts girl.

BARBIE-JEAN stands up and storms off in the direction of the kitchen. KEVIN grabs her arm and stops her.

BARBIE-JEAN: Get off me!

KEVIN: Oh no Barbie; no ya don't. Ya no' doin' one o' your selfish little stormin' off routines! We're no' 'avin' that! Stay and listen!

BARBIE-JEAN: What is there to listen to?

KEVIN: Me! 'Cause I'm telling ya – right, ya mum's no' comin' back. An' I'm not sittin' around all me life waitin' for 'er.

BARBIE-JEAN: Why did she leave in the first place then?

KEVIN: Barbie – listen, for once in ya life stop bein' so fuckin' selfish! You always 'ave to put ya self first!

BARBIE-JEAN: And what do ya think you ever do – and mum. I have to put myself first; no-one else will.

KEVIN: Wha' about what's good for me! Look, as far as your mum's concerned, you an' Jake are grown up now. There's no need to come back, the way she sees it. She was lookin' for any excuse…

BARBIE-JEAN: If Janet moves in – I'm moving out!

KEVIN: Oh yeh. Where to?

BARBIE-JEAN: I'll go to my nan's.

KEVIN: Oh yeh. An' she can afford to put you through university can she, eh?

BARBIE-JEAN sits down. Silence. KEVIN sits on the grass and sips his tea.

You'll be off to university next year. I don't know wha' ya worried about.

BARBIE-JEAN reads the Oscar Wilde book.

'Ave ya spoken to ya mum yet?

BARBIE-JEAN: No. I put the 'phone down. I think though, I've decided, well, I've decided the best thing to do now is to speak to her. That's what Oscar Wilde would do.

KEVIN: Janet's no' stupid ya know. She reads books an' everythin'. You'll ge' on with 'er. You got on alright didn't ya, last time?

BARBIE-JEAN: Yes.

KEVIN: She likes you. An' Jake. She wouldn't move in if she didn't.

Enter JAKE.

JAKE: Auntie Pauline's 'ere.

KEVIN: Where?

JAKE: She's just seein' to the baby.

BARBIE-JEAN: Where have you come from?

JAKE: Me mum.

BARBIE-JEAN: Funny.

KEVIN: Does she need any 'elp?

JAKE: I put 'er bags in the hall.

Enter PAULINE.

KEVIN: Alright. 'Ow do ya ge' from the station?

PAULINE: Go' a taxi.

KEVIN: Thought you were skint.

PAULINE: I am. Alright Barb.

BARBIE-JEAN: Hi.

KEVIN: Should o' called me mobile. I'd 'ave picked you up.

PAULINE: I can't stand around waitin' for a lift when I've got the baby. She was tired.

BARBIE-JEAN: Where is she?

PAULINE: It's alright, she's asleep. She's in 'er pram, in the kitchen.

JAKE: Arh let's 'ave a look.

PAULINE: No. Leave 'er. She's asleep. We don't wan' 'er cryin' again. Once she starts she never shuts up.

BARBIE-JEAN: She's placid, normally.

PAULINE: Used to be. She's teethin' now. Anyway Jake, you'll 'ave enough on your plate bringin' up Stella's baby. (*She laughs.*)

JAKE: It's not mine.

PAULINE: I bet. That's wha' the' all say.

JAKE: It's not. It can't be mine.

PAULINE: You'll 'ave the soshe onto ya soon. Wantin' payments.

JAKE: Shut up. I won't.

PAULINE: I'm only teasin' ya love. (*She ruffles his head.*) Arh – 'e's me favourite you know. You're me little pageboy, aren't ya lad? There 'e was, up the path, ready to 'elp 'is old aunt with 'er suitcases; not like you ugly bastards. Ge' me a drink Jakey babe.

KEVIN: Knew she was after something.

JAKE: Wha' do ya want?

PAULINE: A lemonade'll do darlin'.

JAKE: (*To BARBIE-JEAN and KEVIN.*) I'm no' makin' youse nottin'.

BARBIE-JEAN: I'm so hurt.

KEVIN: These two are still carryin' on – like they're scared o' catchin' something from each other. They've been like this since Torquay – that was three fuckin' months ago.

JAKE exits to the kitchen.

PAULINE: (*Whispering.*) So wha' do ya think like?

KEVIN: Wha'?

PAULINE: Is it Jake's or wha'?

BARBIE-JEAN laughs.

What's funny?

KEVIN: (*To BARBIE-JEAN.*) Nothing's funny. Jake's still sayin' it's not 'is.

PAULINE: It probably 'is in tha' case.

KEVIN: So is that it then?

PAULINE: What?

KEVIN: Are you bringin' tha' baby up now?

PAULINE: 'Er name's Lisa you arsehole.

BARBIE-JEAN: Where's Kerry?

PAULINE: Still in the flat. 'Er fella's nowhere to be found. Knew it wouldn't last. The baby's with me full time still.

KEVIN: Friggin' 'ell. 'Ow do ya ge' out?

PAULINE: I don't do I? That's wha' I come down 'ere for. Barb'?

BARBIE-JEAN: What?

PAULINE: Do ya fancy babysittin' tonight? You're the only person I can trust. I just wanna quick drink with ya dad.

KEVIN: I'm meetin' Janet tonight.

PAULINE: We'll all go out together.

BARBIE-JEAN: I've got an essay to do – on Wordsworth.

PAULINE: Oh 'ave ya? Big fuckin' deal. The baby can 'elp. Look, it's Sundee. Pubs close early. We'll be back by one.

Enter JAKE with PAULINE's lemonade. He hands it to her.

PAULINE: Tar babe.

JAKE: I'll babysit for ya Pauline. But only if Tony can come round.

KEVIN: No chance.

PAULINE: She's alright as long as she's go' 'er bottle.

KEVIN: Yeh. 'E'll probably give 'er a bottle o' cider.

PAULINE: Look, Barbie, if you're gonna stay in to do an essay, just keep an eye on things. Jake an' Tony can sit with 'er. Me an' you can go out tomorra night Barb.

BARBIE-JEAN: Tomorrow? I'm in school.

KEVIN: She's not goin' out durin' the week.

PAULINE: Jesus. I thought life up in Wales was dead borin'
– then I came to visit you shower o' miserable bastards.

KEVIN: We'll just take it easy tonight.

PAULINE: 'Ow do ya mean?

KEVIN: Janet likes a quiet drink, that's all. Nottin' too
rowdy.

JAKE: Can Tony stay tonight then dad?

KEVIN: Yes. I thought you were just round there.

JAKE: I was. 'E was just gettin' up. I'll give 'im a ring.

KEVIN: 'E are – 'ang on.

JAKE and KEVIN exit.

PAULINE: What's up with you then?

BARBIE-JEAN: What?

PAULINE: Don't try an' be smart. Ya know what. You've
not been the same since the 'oliday. What's 'appened to
ya?

BARBIE-JEAN: The holiday – was a disaster. It made me
wake up.

PAULINE: Ya never come to stay any more – Kerry thinks
she's no' good enough for you now. Ya don't even bother
with the baby. Every time I come down you run off an'
'ide. Ya never wanna go out. Why can't ya baby sit then?

BARBIE-JEAN: I told you; I'm otherwise engaged.

PAULINE: Otherwise engaged! Who the fuck are you tryna
impress – 'cause ya sound like a right fuckin' dick 'ead.
Yeh you can sigh girl. Otherwise engaged my arse! Talk
normal will ya?

BARBIE-JEAN: I am talking…normally.

PAULINE: Ya not! You sound fuckin' stupid. Who do you think you are all of a sudden – Penelope fuckin' Keith? To the manor born now are we? Drop the stupid accent – you'll end up getting your fuckin' 'ead kicked in.

BARBIE-JEAN: It's up to me how I talk.

PAULINE: Barbie – you're a fake, right; a fraud. Everything about you is false, includin' ya fuckin' eyelashes.

BARBIE-JEAN: I don't wear those any more.

PAULINE: Oh no of course not. At least you were a good laugh then; at least ya had a sense of humour.

BARBIE-JEAN: You laughed at me, not with me.

PAULINE: No I didn't Barb. I laughed with you. It's now I'm laughin' at you, along with the rest o' the population.

BARBIE-JEAN: What do you know?

PAULINE: You're certainly the clown now aren't ya? You think ya so fuckin' special 'cause you're readin' a few books an' goin' to university, if they're stupid enough to let you in. It's all so false. An' wha' do ya think you're gonna achieve from all this?

BARBIE-JEAN: From all what?

PAULINE: Losin' your accent? Do ya think it'll make you better than the rest of us – is that what you think?

BARBIE-JEAN: No.

PAULINE: My arse ya don't. You big gobshite. It's a very lonely path wha' you're goin' down. You better be very fuckin' careful, 'cause you won't find any love down there, I'll tell ya that for a start.

BARBIE-JEAN: Pauline, I'm just getting an education.

PAULINE: Pauline – oh I'm not ya Auntie Pauline then? 'Course that's too common isn't it? Especially if ya wanna hang out with Tarquin, ya know, when you're otherwise engaged – at university. Wanna learn to tell the difference now do ya, eh, between an expresso an' a cappuccino?

BARBIE-JEAN: Espresso – not expresso.

PAULINE: Whatever. If you think I'm laughin' at you now Barbie-Jean, you wait till you get to know Tarquin just that little bit more, 'cause 'e'll certainly be laughin' at you, wha' with a scally name like Barbie-Jean. You'll be the freak show alright – only difference is, 'e'll laugh at you behind ya back, were as I'll do it to ya face, an' do ya wanna know why? – because I actually care about whether you live or die. Do you think you'll ever ge' any genuine love from them kind o' people, do you think they'll ever really accept you? Wake up Barbie! You'll never be one o' them. You can't change who you are just by changin' ya fuckin' accent – unless you can act non-stop twenty-four hours a day, which I don't think ya can, an' anyway, it'd be a very tedious experience, especially for everyone else.

BARBIE-JEAN: This is paranoia.

PAULINE: Wha' I wanna know is, if it's just an education you want, why do ya 'ave to start talkin' posh? Why are ya tryna 'ide where ya come from? You should be proud o' comin' from Liverpool. It's the birth place o' Ken Dodd an' the Diddy Men.

BARBIE-JEAN: Ken Dodd and the Diddy Men!

PAULINE: That was a joke. You see you 'ave lost ya sense o' humour.

BARBIE-JEAN: No I haven't; and look I'm not hiding anything.

PAULINE: I think you are girl. An' it won't be just your accent you lose, 'cause you won't be one of us anymore, anymore than you'll ever be one o' them. You'll end up a very lonely outsider. I know Barbie – remember I worked in a private school. I might 'ave only cleaned the fuckin' tea trays, but I could see wha' was goin' on. The people in them places, their lives are mapped out for them. They're destined for university – from the day they're born; an' even when they're crap they still ge' the best jobs. Life's just a series o' fuckin' games an' rituals for them. It's the night o' the living fucking dead. But you can never be tha' Barb, 'cause it's not wha' you are, thank God. You'd ge' found out. I bet you think a black tie dinner means people turnin' up wearin' black ties.

BARBIE-JEAN: Yeh.

PAULINE: Now who looks fuckin' stupid? Only thing is, I won't judge you for it. The kind o' people you wanna become like, by now, they've already 'ad their first black tie dinner, never mind findin' out wha' it fuckin' means. It's a uniform – it separates them from the likes o' you an' me. It's a private club Barbie, an' I'm afraid you missed the vital stages of initiation, an' when you get to know them, you'll be grateful. (*Indicating the books.*) They take all this kinda stuff for granted. So, go to university Barbie, an' read ya books, but just don't ever kid yourself. Ya know, the joke is, ya makin' an issue out o' nottin'.

BARBIE-JEAN: I'm making an issue – what are you on about?

PAULINE: There – got ya!

BARBIE-JEAN: What?

PAULINE: Wha' are you on about? – scouse talk that. You said it. See. Slipped already. You won't be able to make tha' kind o' mistake at Lord Radley's dinner party, or every time you lose ya temper.

BARBIE-JEAN sighs.

Barbie – get real. This isn't the sixties. No-one cares about wha' ya sound like. 'Aven't ya seen the news lately? Ya suppose to be educated. Even the newsreaders 'ave accents. They never used to.

BARBIE-JEAN: That's different.

PAULINE: How is it? Grow up Barbie. Ya no' in a fuckin' Oscar Wilde play – talkin' o' social climbin' rejects.

The sound of the baby crying.

BARBIE-JEAN: And what have you got to offer, bringing up babies?

PAULINE: Yes actually.

BARBIE-JEAN smirks.

Fuckin' smirkin' are ya? Wha' do you know about babies eh? In fact wha' do you fuckin' know about anything? Fuck all, so wipe tha' smile off ya fuckin' face!

Enter KEVIN.

Think ya a stakeholder in the fountain of all knowledge now, 'cause you've read a fuckin' book?

KEVIN: What's kicked you off now?

PAULINE: (*Ignoring him.*) Barbie, you've 'ad one fuckin' brother to deal with all ya life, an' you've spent most o' your time walkin' all over 'im.

BARBIE-JEAN: I haven't.

KEVIN: Eh – shut ya fuckin' mouth now you will ya?

PAULINE: I fuckin' won't. She needs be told. Don't you start on me.

KEVIN: Leave 'er alone.

PAULINE: Wha' – like our Angie did?

KEVIN: You're fuckin' way out of order girl.

PAULINE: (*To KEVIN.*) Eh – you ought to know – (*turning back to BARBIE.*) – there were seven of us in my family, seven kids; most o' the time we were scrappin' over food, not who gets to use the fuckin' bathroom! Sometimes we 'ad nottin'. An', ya know wha', it could o' been worse – there should o' been nine kids in my family; nine times my mum got pregnant, but she lost two, an' you wanna know why – I'll tell ya; one night me dad comes 'ome, pissed, as per fuckin' usual – kicked the fuckin' shit out of 'er – kicked 'er down the fuckin' stairs. She 'ad an abortion the next day. An' the other time she lost one, she wasn't getting enough to eat, so don't you fuckin' smirk at me girl about fuckin' babies or nottin', 'cause ‚you know jack shit! You don't know wha' it's like to see ya mum – too embarrassed to go the fuckin' shops 'cause she's got two fuckin' big black eyes. She looked like a fuckin' panda in the greengrocers; it's a wonder she didn't come 'ome with a bag full o' fuckin' bamboo shoots. An' tha' 'appened all the time round 'ere. So fuckin' smirk at me now.

KEVIN: Don't be takin' your frustrations out on 'er, just 'cause you've let ahl arse back in ya life!

PAULINE: Eh; tha' ahl arse just 'appens to be your brother.

KEVIN: No-one forced ya to take 'im in girl; you're stupid enough…

PAULINE: An' your mum – was she being stupid was she, when she put up with ya dad all them years, an' 'e was a right bastard to 'er? 'As it ever occurred to you, the reason she might o' stuck with 'im, is because she actually fuckin' loved 'im? An' if I didn't look after John, no-one else would: I don't see you around much, I don't see you there, when 'e's so drunk, 'e can't even recognise 'is own fucking daughter in the street, an' then 'as to be pulled out of his own pool o' fuckin' piss an' vomit. No-one's there then are the'? I'm on me own.

125

JAKE: (*Off.*) The baby's awake.

PAULINE: (*To JAKE.*) I'm comin' now. (*To KEVIN.*) Can I borrow tha' money or wha' then?

KEVIN: 'Ow much do ya need?

PAULINE: A couple o' 'undred should do – see me over.

JAKE: (*Off.*) Can I pick the baby up?

PAULINE: Be careful. I'm comin' now.

KEVIN: I'll go the bank first thing tomorra.

PAULINE: Tar.

KEVIN: Just make sure 'e doesn't ge' 'is fuckin' 'ands on it.

PAULINE: No chance. I'll put it straight into me account – only place it's safe. I need it for the baby. Can't 'ave tha' fuckin' kid starvin'.

KEVIN: 'Course not.

JAKE: (*Off.*) She's been sick on me 'and!

PAULINE: I'm comin'.

PAULINE exits. BARBIE-JEAN picks up the book of Wordsworth's poetry and reads.

KEVIN: She's a fuckin' pain tha' woman.

Pause. KEVIN picks up the Oscar Wilde book.

Are you still readin' this play thing?

BARBIE-JEAN: Which one – *Lady Windermere's Fan*? No. I finished that ages ago.

KEVIN: Oh yeh? Wha' 'appens then?

BARBIE-JEAN: It's a bit sad.

KEVIN: Yeh?

KEVIN lies down.

BARBIE-JEAN: (*Speaking in a rush and excitedly.*) It's hard to explain. Basically, this girl, right, Lady Windermere, posh names of course, anyway, this woman turns up, Mrs Erlynne, anyway, Lady Windermere thinks she, Mrs Erlynne, is having sex with her husband, Lord Windermere – so she gets all hormonal and starts having an affair with this bloke, Lord Darlington, but she doesn't really; she just thinks about it. That's when it gets interesting – what she doesn't know, right, is that this woman, right, Mrs Erlynne, is actually her mother – Lady Windermere's mother. Not only that, but Mrs Erlynne – she's not even having it off with Lord Windermere. Of course, Mrs Erlynne knows the truth, I mean, about Lady Windermere, about Lady Windermere being her daughter. She knows that. So, anyway, right, Mrs Erlynne, right, sacrifices her own reputation to save her daughter's good name, Lady Windermere that is. But Lady Windermere still thinks Mrs Erlynne is really evil, until the end, right, when she realises that the only bitch is herself. So she forgives Mrs Erlynne, but without realising it's her mother, but if she knew it was her mother, if she knew how her mother really felt deep down inside, she might be happy.

Pause.

Dad?

KEVIN: Yeh?

BARBIE-JEAN: Are you listening?

KEVIN: Yeh.

In fact he is dozing off. BARBIE-JEAN goes back to reading her book. Sound of the baby crying. Blackout.